Stop *Stop* **Stop**

Undust the Common Sense of

TIMELESS WISDOM

Copyright©2015 by Helen Xinhui Zhu and X.H. New Wisdom

All rights reserved. No part of this book may be reproduced, translated into other languages or transmitted in any form or by any means, electronic or mechanical, including photocopying, recording, or by any information storage and retrieval system, without permission in writing from the authors except for brief quotations and reviews for education purposes. The book, first edition, is published in the United States, by Learn with Universal Mind Publishing.

For translation into other languages, please email LWUM at lwumLP@learnwithuniversalmind.com

ISBN 978-0-9892826-8-0

on behalf of
Learn with Universal Mind foundation

In Conjunction with
The United Nations Assembly

All Rights Reserved

November, 2015
Learn With Universal Mind Publishing

Transformational

Initiatives to
The Green Earth Life

A **REAL** Game Changer

All Proceeds of the Book Will Go to the Three Specific Initiatives Proposed in the Book

Initiative 1# No Land Left Dry Global Vegetation Movement

Initiative 9# project1 Sahara Desert Transformation to a Diverse Land of Lakes, Palm Trees, Bushes and Oasis, Forests

Initiative 10# project 3 Life Trees Program, a life time education and engagement for families

CONTENTS

Part I
We Must Aim High, Because We Were Born High

1	Humans Outpace the Nature	7
2	Timeless Wisdom and the Common Sense	15
3	The Common Sense Says to Us: We Must Stop	21
4	The Timeless Wisdom tells us: We Are One	31
5	The Four Principles of the Heavenly Law to Be Upheld in Worldly Affairs to Let Our Common Sense Shine	33
6	Definitions and Conceptual Comprehension Under Green Earth Life	52

Part II Green Earth Initiatives

Holistic Approach for Global Development of Green Economy with an Earth Vision Amidst Climate Change and Environment Devastation

1	I Symbolism	61
2	II Reversion and Conversion Projects	65
3	III Creation Projects	105
4	IV Human Species Management	131
5	Ending	160
6	About Authors	161
7	Reference	162

Part I

We Must Aim High, Because We Were Born High

As Muhammad, the last prophet said: ***"your lives[1] and your property[2] are sacrosanct until you meet your lord..."*** In other words, every human being is born of a sacred being, but one day each of us meets our own lord who may lead us to or discord us from The Sacred Source.

Humans outpace the nature!

"[The foxes have their holes] and the birds have [their] nests, but the Son of Man has no place to lay his head and rest." - Jesus Christ

Millions of people are struggling in wars, billions of marine lives, land animals, and other species are dying, thousands of waters and lakes are turning yellow, black or red, undrinkable, trillions of trees

---

[1] the soul that passes from one body to another in different lives
[2] the body

were uprooted, the forests are burning, the temperature is rising and the land is drying up, the deserts are expanding – in this roaring devastation of reality, the world is awakening, billions of people have recognized the damages humans have done to the nature - the environment where every created being relies on to sustain its life; billions of people start to seek and apply natural solutions for sustainable living and development. However no sustainable system can cope with it if an uncontrollable human activity is set free, which outpaces the rhythm of nature and breaks the natural life circle in this earth environment which is a delicate and finery garden that requires much care to sustain and to flourish. The Sun rises and sets in a 24 hour cycle, the moon sets and rises in a 24 hour cycle; in these 24 hour cycles, days and nights pass, seasons pass, years pass, and space time passes. With these 24 hour cycles in the originally created, natural field, men were naturally supplied with everything we needed, with ease. Animals and plants, other beings know this, they have always been following this natural rhythm, resting and acting, resting more than acting; But men, by chasing after an illusionary promise in our mind, have been striving non-stop troubling the swell minds, busying the heavy hands, toiling the weary and distorted bodies, gradually became slaves on an alien field created by the desires and lust of ourselves for more, for big to several times overdraft of the earth. With men's strife, have been broken many of the natural cycles which were originally situated on a delicate, intangible and sophisticated universal clock; as a result, many strings in the natural clock are broken; Now more and more people are joining the seas of awakening, longing for solutions to jump out of the situations we are bounded in, to undo what we have done.

Is that simply a shift from fossil fuel to solar power for energy supply could rest assure us in resolving all the issues we are facing today? Probably no body would say 'yes' although it no doubt will slow down this trend of devastation. Then where are the solutions?

We say, they are not far in Heaven, they are not very technical either, requiring a genius mind to comprehend, but right in front of our eyes, in an arm's reach if we allow the seal to be opened! And the seal is our own mind!

Many people may have known or heard of the Zamzam well, a miraculous ancient spring well located about 66 feet away from the Kaaba, in Mecca.

Throughout history, the location of the well has been decorated and updated time after time, from a simple, naturally stone-enclosed water well to a structure now housed in the magnificent, luxury Al Haram Complex. Today millions of people each year from all over the world come to pay pilgrimage at Al Haram, they drink the well water, also take some back to friends and relatives, hoping their problems be resolved as well as help bring them to the afterlife. All the emphasis has been focused on the water's miraculous function, however the ancient but timeless wisdom contained in the Zamzam Well story has been completely ignored and buried in the busy life of today's modern civilization.

According to Al-Bukhari's Sahih, after a friction between his two wives, Abraham took his second wife Hagar and his son Ismail to Mecca, and left them sitting under a tree with a skinbag of water, then headed for home. Hagar followed him half way and asked to whom he would leave them, he replied he would leave them to Allah. By hearing that, Hagar felt satisfied going back to her place, started drinking the water and breast feeding her infant child. As Mecca was located in a hot dry valley with few sources of water, when the water in the skin had been finished, she said to herself, "I'd better go and look so that I may see somebody.' She ascended the Safa mountain and looked, hoping to see somebody, but in vain. When she came down to the valley, she ran till she reached the Marwa mountain", ascended Marwa hoping to see anybody, again in vain. Then she ran seven times back and forth between Safa and Marwa to seek, but still found nobody to help. Then she thought 'I'd better go to see what the state of my child', at that moment she heard a voice, it was Angel Gabriel, and he hit the ground with his heel, and a spring water gushed out. Hagar drank and fed her child Ismail with the water. And then fearing the water might run out, Hagar tried to contain the water and repeated the command 'Zamzam' in her attempt of enclosing the spring water. 'Zamzam' originated from 'ZomeZome' meaning 'stop, stop' in Arabic.

It was an aha moment to rediscover the wisdom for us when the meaning of the two mountains in Arabic were revealed with the context of the story. Safa in Arabic means purity and serenity; and Marwa means a fragrant plant which represents something solid in the world that attracts the sense pleasures. So first part of the story tells: Hagar was running between the two mountains of serenity & purity and solid sensual attraction in searching water to satisfy her thirst, and the second part tells: when the spring water was showed to Hagar, she tried to contain it, but naturally cried out 'stop, stop'. Someone said **had Hagar had not contained the spring water, today it would have been flowing the entire earth.**

According to another legend, Abdul Muttalib, grandfather of Muhammad, the last prophet, once had a dream. In the dream he was told to dig Zamzam, but he did not know what was Zamzam, so he asked, and he was replied *'a well that never gets dry to satisfy the thirst of pilgrims. It is located between the points where the offerings are slaughtered; where the crow strokes with its beak'.*

Throughout human history on one extreme, we had numerous sages, spiritual masters who through various paths obtained elevation in spiritual actualization but at the cost of living a life of exclusion from the world, some even could not be self-sufficient to their own body, and how much serenity they had obtained, only they themselves could answer, and the limited number of them may have already been a strong proof that it is unachievable for the masses although they were desperately needed at times in keeping the physical world from being destructed; after all the whole existence would not be a complete demonstration if just the spiritual side of it was realized; then on the other extreme, the whole world has been falling in the trap of pursuing endless material gratification in the form of chasing after money, power, fame, sense pleasures etc. at the cost of disconnection with Spirit, God, causing distortion to the body of individuals, deadly diseases to the backbone of humanity, which have induced quarrels, fights and bloodsheds among humanity, and the lack of coordination in all the worldly affairs. Today our problem is not that we ascended the Safa mountain to have obtained serenity and purity; but we climbed up and occupied and overcrowded the Marwah mountain, and as a result we stepped on, crashed off each other, and caused death and chaos. Our today's problems in climate change, in environmental eco devastation, in political inertia, in human and animal killings, are all the manifestation of our individual and collective discord from the periphery of the Garden where the Creator put us and where we are supposed to walk and play. And unfortunately we are walking in an alien field and this was led by striving along Jacob's path and following Jacob's god.

For the world, our true life, the Eternal Life be nurtured by the Eternal Spring which runs neither from the extremely isolated renunciation from the physical world, which has failed in transforming the world to a much enlightened place, nor from the extreme heavy mass and material aggregation that the whole world has now been trapped in and bring us towards destruction, some may not be even aware of, and some are reluctant to admit, and some intentionally deny or completely lost the ability to recognize because of the massive gravitation and inertia in play in this material world. The Zamzam well, 'It is located between the two offerings, and where the crow strokes with its beak' which mean we need to live a balanced and grounded life that requires our life styles well fit in the nature and governed by the natural universal Law of Balance between Yin and Yang energies[3].

We must aim high, because we were born high; we were born meant to walk, some of us could fly, but we are crawling; by crawling, we mean human beings have been striving to contain everything, possess everything and control everything which be under the care of other species, other life forms governed by the Natural Law, and which immensely burdens our mind, distort our body, and altered our genes, and as a result the whole natural eco-systems have been altered, the pure and serene relationships in this Eternal Family have been trampled under our own feet, and now we are paying the prices to what we have done to them.

It is time for us to stand up and learn to fly! We are Sons of God. Our God nature was seated in each of us when we were born, but as a mirror always be sit by dusts if not cared of, we have been unconsciously, through thousands of years, allowing all the worldly, ungodly equity sit on and wrapped up our Spirit, like a yoke clinched on our neck, in the forms of endless desires, greed and lust embedded in all our social endeavors in the phenomena of inequality, divisiveness, separation, deprivation, indifference, cynicism, endless competition, exploitation,

---

[3] *reference: the Book "2 in 1 in 2 the Supreme Revelation"*

selfishness, cruelty, violence, then escalated to wars and killings of our kindred and animals. And all these are of negative energies that have been hovering over our head and depositing in our body, thickly wrapping up and dusting our Spirit. Without Spirit shining, our body is like a corpse, dead; without Spirit shining, it is like a seriously wounded host that cannot move, hopelessly watching parasites consume its body; **God has given us nothing in this physical world as our property but our body, it was the pure manifestation of His Great Wealth in this physical world.** Our time in this physical realm is to live with ease instead of toilsome, to enjoy His entire creation by looking after it and manifesting His creation intention in each of us through looking after our own body, safeguarding it from being dusted, from being enslaved to endless worldly desires, keeping it as pure as it is, the God Nature!

Timeless Wisdom and the Common Sense

Timeless Wisdom tells us, the Eternal life is the water stream sprung out from the efforts living between the worldly life and the pure God Consciousness. The Lust of money and power, self gratification is destroying the world; it is the darkness energy that many of us unconsciously accept to sit in our body and allow our body to become its host. The most sacred and pure place is in our heart, and if this place is tainted, if the heart of humanity is tainted, there is nowhere to be left in the world as pure as Holy, as beautiful as natural!

We must STOP the current trends of chasing money and profit, stop striving for possession, for containing; these concepts cause separation and waste, make us slaves, blind us to see the light, seal us from opening our mind to infinite possibilities to the Eternal Life. We came to this world empty, we can bring nothing from this world except our own soul when we leave. So do you want to be a chained soul or a liberated one when you leave this world?

Jesus said: *become passers-by*!

We must safeguard our body, the host of God, the house, the temple and the city of Spirit, undust excessive worldly desires, lest it is too late before we meet our second death.

As many of us have already woken up and sensed the urgency of our situation on earth, also many of us are still tightly bounded to the material chain; it is time for us all to shake off the dusts, let our Spirit shine.

To move towards the Safa mountain, to raise the vibration of humanity, we need to help each other by pulling, pushing and watching out for each other, as Jesus said: *"Love your brother like your soul, guard him like the pupil of your eye."*

Our God Nature is unconditional love, universal brotherhood in the qualities of equality, wholeness, unity, compassion, giving, generosity, cooperation, nurturing, selflessness, kindness, love and peace; in other words, **Love Yourself, Love Others, Love God** are the three aspects in life we must set right when we are in this physical world. We are all God's children, a member of His Eternal Family no matter what culture or religion backgrounds you come from. God nature, God consciousness naturally empowers us with our **common sense**; this common sense means we would always engage in seeking a balance to nurture the three relationships with God, with others and with ourselves.

- This common sense tells us when we have to make between choices in our individual life, we would not sacrifice the life of our son, our brother, our friend in order to obtain God's favor; instead we would rather offer a hundred sheep off of our own belongs

- This common sense tells us in doing 'business', when someone's roof is leaking, we offer our services for hundreds of dollars to repair it other than for thousands of dollars to tear the whole roof off and replace it with a new one, only because we want to earn more money or we want to give our employees more work to do

- This common sense tells us when we have to make decisions on public policies, we would first consider we are earth citizens, we are human beings living in this earth environment which is a big family instead of our culture, our country, our group, just because we want to protect our immediate interests to gain glory, praise, fame, greatness and power, so that we could formulate harmonious development policies that would benefit the whole circle of life with ease in the earth environment instead of depriving and wasting resources

- This common sense tells us, when we have enough food and clothes, we would not want more, buy more only because they are on sale so that we can avoid either distorting our own body or giving chances to depletion of the shared environment

- This common sense tells us, on a scorching hot day if we are outside, we would like to stay in the shade of a tree to feel the fresh and cool air other than walking or driving on a bald road without any protection from the sun; we would feel the several degree differences in the air temperature, and naturally we would want to grow more trees in our environment instead of fewer.

- This common sense again tells us, water is life, it is more precious than anything else, without water there is no life to start and to survive, therefore we would sacrifice our lives to protect the waters rather than letting them being polluted, nor letting money or profit have a say over its fate.

- This common sense also tells us, if our brothers or sisters fall in a well, we would try everything to help them up instead of throwing stones in the well, only because we fear they would later come up to compete with us!

And these are the **quality of love**, the **quality of simplicity** and the **quality of softness**, of the God nature in its daily expressions. Any qualities in contrast of these ones are ungodly, they are the destructive forces driving us away from where we want to go, and they are in the way for us to return to our Eternal Family. And only when our individual life and collective social life are engaged in obtaining these qualities, and make these qualities, instead of money and self-gratification, the pursuit in our daily life, then our environment will be surly transformed towards the center of the two offerings – that is the Green Earth Life, the heavenly field where we belong to; and these are particular true for those individuals in power who are held responsible for decision-making on public policies.

We must also make clear that when we talk about God nature, we do not mean religion; when we quote some ancient scriptures for timeless wisdom, we do not mean culture, but we mean Spirit. God is the Supreme Spirit, God is All That IS, we are sparks of Its Light. The Timeless Wisdom has been passed on to all humanity in parts on a thread of God's Salvation by Words at different ages through different individuals with different backgrounds. That does not mean the people who were given the messages have any privilege over other people, it only means that the Timeless Wisdom cannot be contained by any group, any nation, any culture nor any religious group, and it is free available for all men to access as the guidance on the journey to return to the Eternal Home. History has already proved whoever attempts to do the opposite has to pay retribution and would be cast under the wheel of space time, which can only bring bloodshed to humanity.

Look at today's world, the inequality of material wealth does not only exist in USA, in UK , in all capitalist countries, but also exist in China, in India, in Russia, in Africa, in Latin America and in all socialist countries; it is in fact a common phenomenon that has existed for thousands of years in any social political systems and it has been magnified to its extremity since the last 200-300 years ago when the money games became bigger and more complicated; the civil injustice adheres to any society, not just in the east, but also in the west, in the north and the south; climate change, environmental devastation do not just happen in a particular part of the world, they follow wherever human's foot sets on, wherever modern commercial operations reach.

Hence the common sense says to us: We Must Stop

Today the struggle of humanity is not a struggle between rich and poor, east and west, north and south, neither a struggle between any 'isms', but it is a struggle for liberation of the human's body from mind to heart, a struggle from separation to reunion, a struggle from divisiveness to unity. When we think too much, we blindly dig well ('wealth') for ourselves, try to hold for ourselves, to quarrel, to fight each other off; When we think too much we blindly bury our heads playing games, and the games get bigger and bigger till we cannot handle them ourselves; as a result we have been adamantly shot off the ground and out of touch of the green field and feel too little; when we feel too little, our hearts become tighter and tighter till we cannot feel the softness, the subtleness of life surround us; our souls have been oppressed to diminish till we cannot sense anymore the common sense that the timeless wisdom has bestowed us, which emanates from our precious souls.

Thus when we become awakened, we may suddenly

realize that the nature is calling us to stop what we have been doing, especially in the specific three habitual deeds:

- Stop striving in any endeavors in any worldly affairs, be in 'politics', in 'economies', in 'individual' or in 'social' life, to take a break, to slow down and check the map for bringing us back to the Eternal Home. You do not need to strive at any cost in order to obtain your set goals or your desires for a particular outcome, instead after you set your motion for a quality of life, you may step back and take care of it with ease, with gentleness; If what you are doing fits in the bigger picture which is governed by the natural Law of Balance, by the Providence, everything will fall in shape; if not after some trials, you would need to get prepared and open yourself for a different approach, do not stick yourself to a particular form. The human's history so far is the result of our resistance to listen to the voice of our souls; therefore we missed the subtle meanings of life! Without the soul to issue the guidance, our flesh body is deemed overdoing, and always goes off track, which has been proved by the bloodsheds of human's striving history. Now it is starting to change with billions of souls awakening. And the Nature is telling us we need to revert this trend and act quickly now, with ease! We hope one day the word 'strive' will vanquish from human's vocabulary completely!

- Stop interpreting ancient scriptures and trying to act into matching events and prophecies if you cannot discern the truth. Today the tragedy of the world is partially the result of misinterpretation of scriptures by some who act blindly or intentionally for their selfish agenda, and partially the result that the mind of the world is willingly being chained and dragged by these misinterpretation. The ultimate interpretation and understanding of scriptures should be checked by their original meanings of the wording set in the energy world. Besides, the scriptures have also been corrupted throughout the ages for various reasons, weeds were sowed along seeds in them including the Book of Revelation.

A dialogue between Jesus and his disciples can tell you the truth:

Disciples: *"Twenty-four prophets spoke in Israel, and all of them spoke in You."*
Jesus: *"You have omitted the one living in your presence and have spoken (only) of the dead."*

No matter what meaningful or holy undertakings we are engaged in, without restraining from strife, we cannot anchor our mind in a resting frequency which is the gateway for us to receive the subtle meanings of life and nature, and this is why humanity has been blocked out at the east to the Garden of Eden by the cherubim; It is also the explanation why Abdumuttalib, the grandfather of Prophet Muhammad placed the two golden reindeers on the door of the Kabaah and made the seal and the key of the Kabaah from gold. In other words, it is our own strife for material wealth and self-gratification and chasing the surface meaning of life that have blocked us to opening the door to Kabaah and to entering the heavenly Garden, and the key to open the door and the entrance is also our mind.

- Stop playing money games. Money, one of the accounting tools, from the beginning of its introduction was utilized just in the trade of products till today it plays deadly important roles in every corner of human's life and it in fact becomes the master of the human body in this commercially dominated world. Just think about it, for a human to survive in the nature he needs water, food and shelter (may include clothes), and the nature actually provides all these already provided the human body is healthy to use his hands to labor, a not very harsh labor. But today it seems without money in the commercially run human society we cannot survive, even if you have some money, a lot of rules, regulations, policies that manage the societies are controlled by those who have big money even though you have a healthy body with two hands to work for living, isn't it odd that money becomes a tool of depriving man's innate ability? And in many injustice social encounters, money can buy a 'win' by replacing the retribution for the violation of justice. No wonder corruption, inequality and injustice exist everywhere in every society in today's world. But if we do not allow money rule our society, rule our body we can change it. And our soul, a part of the Supreme Spirit, which is the true ruler of our body surely does not allow this trend go on forever! The recent melting down of stock markets shows a very clear picture on how the nature wants us to go and how humans resist it! Just simply ask: Even if the stock value of the whole world markets is wiped away to zero in one day, do the world material storage, capacity of production and service reduce suddenly? Not really, except by fear to trigger some reactions in the 'economic' circle. Do the 5 billion pairs of hands (those older than 15 years old) get paralyzed because of the fall of stock markets? And if the trillions of dollars lost in that one day on stock markets have got invested in projects for ecosystems recovery, ie. forestation, other vegetation, land and wildlife recovery, clean water preservation, and green infrastructure building etc. just in 5 years you can imagine how big difference you will be able to see for sure?

We must admit our body has its limitations, clinging to be conditioned to the physical existence, however our soul tells us we are infinite beings, no boundary, we can live beyond our body's limitations, make our body, mind and soul in full alignment; and when we are aware that 'money' becomes a vehicle to carry us to a cliff and to amplify our body's weakness and limitations, distort it, our common sense would tell us that this vehicle needs to be brought under control and may be abandoned one day if necessary.

Jesus said "Blessed is the lion which becomes man when consumed by man; and cursed is the man whom the lion consumes, and the lion becomes man." 'lion' is the lust in human's body for power, for money, for self gratification, in today's world it particularly refers to the lust for money, please refer "2 in 1 in 2 The Supreme Revelation" for elaboration[4].

The money games have changed the genes of human's body and the central nervous system of humanity, hence the Godhead nature of human beings has been

---

[4] Page 104,105

replaced by that of a lion's head or a lion's body, and the whole humanity lost its ability in coordination in all the worldly affairs.

We must stop the mind games, and come down from the Mount Zion

We must come down to find a resting place from the Mt. Zion, a dry mountain, a fortress we have built for ourselves through thousands of years. It is an extension to the Marwah mountain, and it sits above the city of David, a wandering soul. Without a resting place for our heads, our souls will keep wandering following our flesh ancestors, to the deserts.

From the beginning of the creation till the pass-away of the last Prophet Muhammad, humanity had been sent coded messages of the Upper, Middle and Lower three pathways[5] for its development through God's five cardinal incarnations and messengers, i.e. Krishna,

---

[5] *In Pure God Consciousness, they are just three different possibilities, there is no difference and preference as for upper, middle or lower positions; These three labels are the reflections of the duality state in human's mind which views everything in hierarchical structures and sits on a linear vicinity; however the three different possibilities do lead to different experiences for the fleshes in this manifested world*

Laozi, Buddha, Jesus and Muhammad, the last Prophet for Divine Knowledge, the Supreme Law, the Supreme Tool, the Supreme Aid, and the Last Reminder; and all the three pathways had been foretold in Bhagavad Gita, which suggested human beings could choose to arise above the duality mind world and let the Divine knowledge burn away all the material hunkering to reach the Divne Abode as the upper way; or follow two practical approaches as the middle way, the empirical and devotional service, and in later history God sent His two cardinal incarnations Laozi and Buddha to exemplify the two approaches respectively; unfortunately humanity took the lower heavy mass of strife pass and continued mis-perceiving God's Messages by human's mind striving led by the Almighty Lord, single Yang Energy[6].

Only If the lion in human's mind is slain, then our lions in this physical world will survive the slaying!

Only If the desert in the heart of humanity is converted, then the deserts in this world will stop expanding, and converted to oasis!

Only if the lion's body changes to a lamb's, then the door behind the Sphinx will utterly open, and then the dead will arise!

- X.H. New Wisdom

---

[6] page 55, part II of "2 in 1 in 2 the Supreme Revelation"

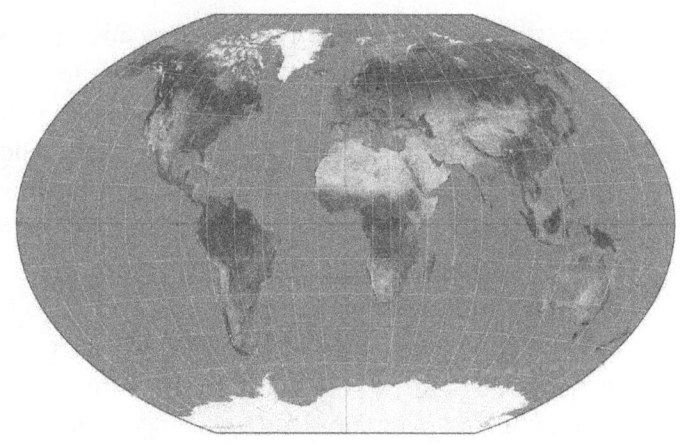

Wikipedia

Today we have two types of aggression – physical violence and tech abuse which have brought bloodshed and hardship to ourselves. Both our body and the technology are wealth and gifts from God to humanity, but we did not use them wisely and safeguard them from falling into an alien field. And both happenings are powered by the mind and carried away by money, which have brought us onto these deserts.

Just look at the geographic map of the world – one of the two most striking desert locations is North Africa

and the Middle East where human activities originated and it has been striven by all kinds of violence and wars throughout history. According to research and study, the Sahara desert used to be covered by a largest fresh Mega lake on earth some 6000 years ago, and completely dried out by just 1000 years ago in a course of a few thousand years; the second upcoming desert starts from California extending to the Midwest of United States. This is a strikingly fast development and high warning: in the last a few years California continues experiencing severe drought, lake level gone down drastically, snowpack run low. If you have read about Lewis and Clark expedition or any early expeditions to the west of North America which happened just over some 200 years ago and described a landscape of rivers, endless forest and vegetation roamed with excitingly large herds of buffalos and elks, bears and other wild animals, you would be astonished by how fast the destruction human beings brought to our delicate garden. And before Silicon Valley gradually was formed, the area used to be orchid farms, and now it becomes compacted with high tech 'giants' who strive to bring out new generations of things to fill the 'convenience of life' in a dazzling fast pace which has lost the true meaning of life. Remember the manifestation of the physical environment in front of our eyes would always come into being first in the energy world.

Put down the 'weapon' in your mind and heart, instantly you can transform to a Buddha

Today

With billions of souls awakening, we declare the winepress of the fierceness and wrath of the Lord Almighty are treaded under our feet;

With billions of spirits arising, we declare the yoke on our neck has been broken to pieces by our hands;

With billions of hearts softening, we declare from the mind to the heart has entered our liberation after 2000 years of struggles and hardship

Today with this mass awakening we realize that we do not have to follow through the rest of the lower pathway described in the scriptures we have unconsciously undertaken for the development of our human race because we are awakened souls who have stood up from the crawling position and whose vision can reach the green pasture where we belong to; a pasture that lies between the Safa and Marwah mountain, a resting place between serenity, purity and fragrant sense pleasure, the Green Earth Life; and it is expanding rapidly, soon it will extend under our feet if we fix our gaze on it and join the billions to work towards it!

The Timeless Wisdom tells us: We Are One

Although quoting Mr. William Bradford here is not an endorsement of any of the author's beliefs and pursuits, we do applaud his profound perception of the Providence and the religious settings: *And I may not omit here a special work of God's providence. There was a proud and very profane young man, one of the sea-men, of a lusty, able body, which made him the more haughty; he would always be contemning the poor people in their sickness and cursing them daily with grievous execrations, and did not let to tell them, that he hoped to help to cast half of them overboard before they came to their journey's end, and to make merry with what they had; and if he were by any gently reproved, he would curse and swear most bitterly. But it pleased God before they came half seas over, to smite this young man with a grievous disease, of which he died in a desperate manner, and so was himself the first that was thrown overboard. Thus his curses light on his own head; and it was an astonishment to all his fellows, for they noted it to be the just hand of God upon him....* [7]

We are undivided, we are One; whoever wants to seek supremacy, domination over his brothers and sisters in whatever forms, or over his cousins (other species), whoever causes separation and divisiveness, whoever wants to rise and exalt as God, he is a false prophet,

---

[7] Excerpt from *"Of Plymouth Plantation"* by William Bradford

he is blasphemy of God, he is against God Nature; By God's will, he may have a temporary place on earth, but there is no peace to him, he will soon face the final judgment of the Providence, and he will be thrown into the lake of fire, destroyed, and this is the law of retribution.

If you ask who we are, here are the answers –

We are Israel, children of God with His Will prevailing, we are not Jews,
We are Muslim, bodies who surrender to the Oneness God, we are not Arabs,
We are Brahmins, sparks of the Supreme Cosmic Spirit, we are not Hindis.

And we are all Souls of Yin Yang twined energies in One Unity.

The Four Principles of the Heavenly Law to Be Upheld in Worldly Affairs to Let Our Common Sense Shine

'After a thousand says and ten thousand talks, action is still our last focus', similar saying 'we cannot just talk the talk, we also need to walk the walk' if we are truly sincere about the survival of our species and sense the urgency of our situation on earth; if we want to see a true change happening from the roots, and if we want to head back towards our Eternal Home; we cannot just 'decapitate one or two Hydra's nine heads to leave chances for them double back', which is what we have been doing so far in resolving the issues the world is facing, and which is doomed in vain; instead we would have to work from the roots to start anew, to change the blood creating cells of our backbones. And we say: Yes, We Can!

To return to the pasture – the Green Earth Life, to regain our God Nature, we would need to comply in all worldly affairs with the Heavenly Law expressed in the four principles which were instituted to humanity by the Creator, and they were encoded in the descriptions of the four rivers in Garden of Eden in chapter 2, Genesis. [8]

When we live in spirit, the expansion of our consciousness would enable us to see not only every individual human beings, individual animals, plants, organism, individual groups, countries, regional groups, cultures, planets, space objects as independent beings, but also be aware of the much intricate relationships between all these units or beings if we view them in spirit; and we realize that we all live in a space time which is situated on an infinite, intricate, unlimited dimensional sphere where everything connects with everything else; and if one thing motions, it would send vibrations and form

---

[8] *Reference: 2 in 1 in 2 The Supreme Revelation, Part 2, p68*

ripple effects to its surrounding beings, and to the entire world and universe; Hence the way of the behaviors of each us individuals, groups matters to the whole, and we would take caution to live our life, to make group decisions. Then the Four Principles of the Heavenly Law would be the new binding laws for the behaviors and activities in a much enlightened world and a fullness of life for individual human beings, individual groups and the whole humanity so that they would guide us to cherish a new age of relationships among all beings living on this beautiful, generous and forgiving Mother Earth, a Great Being that nourishes Life and Wisdom from its Blue Water and Eternal Spirit.

Law of Balance is the Ultimate Heavenly Law to govern the entire universe and its four binding principles permeates in all its textures, subspheres to make the whole system function orderly, as in the ecosystem of the entire life circle on earth, in human society and in individual human body which are the three immediate spheres human beings dwell in

The Four Principles

1. Abundance of Life Forms
    1) unlimited biological lives such as humans, animals, plants, fungi; unlimited non-biological lives such as air, water, soil, rocks, mountains, objects in the universe

Traditional view about life recognized animated organism. With human's consciousness evolving, we have also recognized now inanimate objects as a type of life because their body structure at cellular level, even molecular level would change depending on its environment some of which may not be visible by the naked eyes or in a short time. For instance, the soil would change its structure with the course of no rainfall to it for an adequate long time and with excessive exposure to the sun and it eventually becomes dry land, then erodes to sand, then to desert. And we know now the soil actually contains a lot of organism visible or invisible to the naked eyes which are of subcircles of life in the soil.

Our environment devastation is the result of our ignorance in the past about the life diversity in the ecosystems on earth. When human beings recognize we as one species are one bloc on this sophisticated life circle with an entrusted managing role by the Creator, instead of a master of the circle, our relationship with the nature would be improved and we would be able to rebuild our relationship with the nature in a responsible way through implementing new policies in all projects in worldly affairs.

2) unlimited types and models of a social entity in human society, such as culture, economy, political governance, religion, philosophy, ideology when the entity is viewed in spirit;

Similar to any species in the earth life circle, if we take one species out and study, examine it we enter into one of the subspheres of the earth life. So human society is the subsphere for our human species to live in, and within which all social entities we recognize can be viewed as life forms if we agree there is the Sprit (life) in human society. And this category of life forms has been ignored or not recognized by and large so far in the world. When we start to view culture, economy, political governance etc as life forms, it will not be difficult for us to allow and apply the principle of diversity of life in our social encounters, as in economical models, social political models in managing the human society in different countries and in different stages of development in the same country, and when we allow and accept different models coexist in governance, we would truly appreciate the diversity of approaches which is the abundance of life forms manifested by the Creator's opulence and it will become easier for us to adapt to new models and understand those that are different from ours as long as we all hold dear of our God Nature, the quality of life, our core value of the Sprit. And when our focus is placed on the quality of life instead of the forms of life, our energy will flow to nurture our spirit which would eventually grow into maturity, then the softness, healthiness and colorfulness of life will flow out of us.

In Garden of Eden as describing the first branch of the four, when the water of life springs out and flows over the whole land of the circular, all lives on the land gets nurtured, and the land is good, there are gold (softness), bdellium (healthiness), onyx stone (colorfulness), life would be full of softness and tenderness, healthiness, colorfulness.

2. Unconditional Love -

In God's consciousness, everything is pure existence, there is no preference, division or separation; Sand and gold are equally useful in their respective functionality in His whole creation, neither is favored nor unfavored. An animal and a human being, a sage and a beggar are all spirits in God's Eye and equally taken care of by the dews and sun rays sent by Him from Heaven; In human's perception we call this undivided love of God nature 'unconditional love'.

As seeds of God, when we talk about unconditional love in human society, we mean it is a balanced love between these three aspects of loving yourself, loving your brothers and sisters, and loving God, the Creator as mentioned in previous section. Without a balance between these three, we may favor one and treat another contemptuously which will surely lead us to discord in worldly affairs. An awe respect towards the Creator can restrain us from stepping up and violating the Nature's Law therefore cause sufferings to all beings although in long term the Law would rectify it by its own nature of balance; and a love towards ourselves would ensure that we know who we are and have the gravitational center in our body to always hold ourselves steadfast from being carried away by the perishable worldly events and material gains; and loving brothers and sisters is something seriously missing in our society and needs to be sought back in order to ensure we have a healthy human society where every members of the society are taken care of and living an ease and peaceful life.

And we need to hold high that this undivided love of God Nature towards all brothers and sisters, no matter in what race, culture, nation, what social condition or belief, which emanates from the soul in the Spiritual realm, cannot be differentiated by any conceptions originated from the human's mind in the physical realm.

This unconditional love is based on the understanding that we are of the same Spirit at the core but out of God's Opulence can have different appearances, culture origins, different views about many things which may cause some unease in social encounters, social undertakings; and it would be much pleasant experiences for us to tackle issues if we try to hold a positive view about the motive of others and keep an appreciative attitude towards the differences we have, which may enable us to see more and find new fitting solutions or approaches, and this attitude and approaches apply to both individuals and groups.

As also we are flesh beings in this physical world, who have emotions and feelings that would always bounce back from the solid social formulation. The principles of the Heavenly Law further institutes some norms and codes in the human society which require people living in it abide by; if those norms and codes are violated, it would cause from social unease to extreme disorder. To respond properly, to avoid endless, blind reactions which could only lead to more conflicts and more destructive actions, compassion and forgiveness are the two qualities we would always want to nourish under unconditional love.

However it is easy to show compassion and forgiveness to someone we love and who is our friend, it is not the same to show this attitude and feelings to someone who has done harm to us, may even threatens our own survival (this does not refer to the delusion created by the fear from our own mind). In this situation compassion and forgiveness have their broader meanings.

Compassion and forgiveness to someone who know not what they do

Most of the situations when harms done they came out of someone who are blindly seeking their own interests and advantages driven by their own desires, and they do not know what they have done to others eventually will come back to them which may not be in exactly the same form, because the Supreme Law of Balance is always there. When Jesus said 'Father, Forgive them, they know not what they do', He truly meant 'they know not that they are Sons of God', for if they had known, that knowingness would have activated the code in their DNA, which would in turn generate the Blood of God that bears God Nature to flow in their body, which would always be in readiness to show their understanding, gentleness, compassion and to seek balanced actions in their deeds, they would not have inflicted harms onto Jesus.

By showing compassion and forgiveness, first we release ourselves from anger and possible retaliation which can trigger more undesirable reactions that make our living environment more unease, more chaotic, disturbing other beings in the interwoven environment, our life departing from peace and harmony; and by showing compassion and forgiveness, we do not deprive the offenders of the chance for apology, for correction on their wrong doings. When both sides become aware of the wrongs and have released the energy of destructive forces, there is much chance and room for constructive energy to flow into both sides hence leading to constructive actions; besides, because of the Law of Balance, nothing happens for nothing. When something happens, it always has its meaning in it for us, so ask: what messages the Creator sends to me (us), what can I (we) achieve from the infliction – after you have got the meanings, messages, thank that party who played that role to have made this awareness possible; and this can be made in person or in silence to the Divine.

Compassion and forgiveness to someone who live in complete darkness

In this physical world, there are a small proportion of people who, for various reasons, mainly caused by lust, anger and greed, have completely sunk into the bottom pit of the darkness, become the lowest among men; the Spirit in them is completely, thickly wrapped and buried by the heavy dense material gains. According to Bhagavad Gita, propelled by pride, arrogance, conceit, anger, harshness and ignorance, they completely lost in themselves, lost intelligence, they do not know what is to be done and what is not to be done, there is no truth in them, they actually take falsehood as truth, their actions are madness, they completely mix up righteousness and wrongdoings, they have no feelings while doing harm to other people, other beings, they may deceive hardly leaving any trace, they have the ability to stir up and make confusions among people, and they are only engaged in abhorrent work which is meant to destroy others and the world, they are like cancer cells in the body of humanity. These are the men who completely lost their ability to discern the truth and the false.

When we have encounters with these people, we may even need to show more compassion and forgiveness for the purposes of releasing our own anger and freeing us from undesirable reactions. And forgiveness does not mean the wrongdoers can be exempt from taking responsibilities of their deeds, since the law of retribution under the Supreme Law of Balance is always at work no matter at what space time; so any deeds, and any thoughts derive outcomes and consequences. And since these wrongdoers have lost their ability to recognize and to make correction of their wrongs on their own, it would oblige us and the society to let them know what they are doing is wrong, unacceptable, injustice through appropriate means guided by the four principles of the Heavenly Law, including making them pay retribution, in addition to giving them a chance to make the correction. And these appropriate means shall be made for the aims of correction and helping unlock the chains around their mind and heart instead of punishment and retaliation. Since what we are dealing with is not the body, but the cancer cells caused by the condensed dark energy in the body; if we give punch on them, they would gain more force and split to more and spread more cancers. The cancer cells can only be treated and prevented from spreading by restoring the immune system which would generate new bloodstream to produce healthy cells. **That is to say we need to check our existing social systems and identify the parts which have produced these 'cancers' and replace them with new fresh systems with life.** And this may be the best practice of Jesus saying *"Love your brother like your soul, guard him like the pupil of your eye."* Here love and compassion are expressed in an educational and introspective approach, instead of tenderness which may indulge the wrongdoings and may not lead to the desired results of correction.

And for the 'victims', the showing of forgiveness and compassion does not have to be in person through physical encounter in order to avoid unnecessary eruption of emotions which may trigger undesirable situations; it is in fact much more effective if this is done through sending the thoughts and wishes by the Spirit Self. When the water of life bursts forth without any obstacles, God's unconditional love sheds on all His creations from above, the darkness around humanity would be dissolved by the light shining out from all awakened souls, and the life on earth would be becoming more relaxing, more joyful...

3. Equality and Freedom

As all created beings by God, The Creator are foremost spirit beings having taken different forms in bodies. And as a human being, the individual soul, a quiet observer dwelling in a flesh body, having been encoded with the Heavenly Law, is part of the infinite Super Soul, the Supreme Spirit, God, the Creator, the All That Is through which the individual human souls are connected to each other. While the flesh body, which contains the mind, the senses and the intellect and centered around the mind, is always in constant interaction with the world and easily pulled by the world awry from the soul, which is the gravitational center of the body, directed by the mind. The fall of humanity into the duality state was the sign that the Law of Balance was also broken led by that Single Yang energy in human's body, and a new tedious complicated law in the name of God's Commandments instructed with negative words which guaranteed a stray path was imposed on humanity and from then on through thousands of years it has been spreading negativity to the world and burdening the mind of humanity. However from then on, humanity has also been prescribed a Divine mission that is to break free the old Covenant to regain our Freedom from all the bondages we had been through from physical to mental to spiritual aspect. And this is a journey of liberation from the mind to the heart.

The core concept of freedom in God Nature contains two aspects:

1) freedom for moving around physically, accessing food, water, air and natural shelter for physical health and sustain the body

History tells us when the two basic God Nature – simplicity and oneness (undividedness) were present, it would make possible the freedom of all beings to access all the resources available, but when complicated rules, division, segregation and separation started appearing, which were brought by possession and hoarding, freedom could only be a reach to some, parts of the whole, but was jeopardized for the rest, thus equality simply was impossible.

2) freedom for speech, opinion expression, belief to maintain spiritual wellbeing

Everything is energy. Human's body is solid energy, and speech, opinion and belief are illusive, soft, transformable energy. When these energies are formed in a body, they would need to be expressed, released or transformed into other forms of energy through interaction with other people, other beings or the environment. If freedom for maintaining spiritual wellbeing is blocked, there would be distortion to the body, and they would transform into other types of energy seeking for release, like violence; if there is no channel available for the release of these energies, damage would occur to the body, in the form of illness physically, mentally and psychologically. The way of our human society having been developed simply accumulates too much pressure on everybody in the society from the 'lowest' on the street to the 'highest' in the governing line, from worrying if there is food available the next day to how to keep the authority stable and long; we can say nobody in today's world has true freedom. A situation may be worth for everyone in our society pondering: Sometimes when Helen takes her dog for a walk on streets passing an unfenced big yard, the dog simply wants to stop and roll on that green yard, but Helen has to pull the stubborn dog off the yard in fear of someone rushing out and shouting her away from their property; sometimes she felt so sorry when she saw the innocent and begging look of the dog, she murmured to the dog: "umm, you probably think 'why sometimes I can't stop to play, but sometimes I can, they are all green grass which I like?', why you humans are so complicated?"

The struggle of human history, the problems in today's world are simply because all the qualities, the principles of God Nature were lost on the course of human development, and as spiritual beings, humanity has been fighting for the freedom, first from physical, then to mental, now enter into spiritual state. Before now the struggles of humanity had been blindly guided only by the mind which inclined to overdoing, but when the souls are awakened, we would be able to see more and feel more and listen to the inner voice which comes from God, then the journey for the rest of the liberation from now on would be in ease and enjoyable and harmonious.

Equality and freedom are two of the four principles of the Heavenly Law, the descriptions of them in the scripture were short but put in one verse which implies that equality and freedom are two principles dependent on each other, could not be separated, and they should always be applied at the same time in an orderly world when stipulating any policies and executing any actions. Otherwise It would cause injustice, induce social unease, uprising if either of them is overlooked or ignored because Spirit has no boundary and it always tries to break through any restrains and achieve balance for the whole.

For instance in the case of an overplayed freedom in the market, the current free world market which is mainly operating, organized by money and driven by profit accumulating itself to form a gigantic swirl which sucks in and destroys many other things such as environment, the care about other people and animals, the moral value of God nature because there is not another sufficient force placed onto it to balance it for the gracious purpose for the whole. Because of the nature of capital accumulation it does give freedom to those who hold the capital however it deprives the freedom of equal play of other people who do not have the capital and it causes severe violation of the Divine Law of Balance therefore lead to civil discord and social unrest. The most vital damage it caused is the distortion of the human body that strays from its spirit; when the collective body of humanity strays from the spirit, the three relationships with God, with oneself and with brothers and sisters are messed up and disposed, become upside down, then the Eternal Love of the Eternal Family is destroyed. According to Bhagavad Gita, when the Eternal Family is destroyed, unwanted population is born, ***"An increase of unwanted population certainly causes hellish life both for the family and for those who destroy the family tradition…By the evil deeds of those who destroy the family tradition and thus give rise to unwanted children, all kinds of community projects and family welfare activities are devastated"***[9]

On the other hand if equality is overly emphasized in a society, the free flow of resources would be restrained and the whole social activity may be obstructed. Freedom would always be needed to keep things moving forward and start from points, parts, and meanwhile or short after another force would always be required to enter and make sure the outcomes benefit the whole. In the case of the world economy, national governments, United Nations as the overseeing body of the earth community, regional nation associations, international institutions would need to work together and play the roles of another force in policy making to make sure all beings on earth are beneficial from human's activity.

---

[9] more elaboration in Chapter 1, "2 in 1 in 2 the supreme Revelation" Part II, p15-18

In the case of an ill placed equality, as between men and women in fulfilling their social roles in their daily life, the freedom and beauty of enjoying the diversity of life forms will lose and the original and basic characteristics of men and women may lose. For instance, as a woman is physically less strong built she traditionally avoids taking heavy labor work at home or in the society, but there is the trend and fact in the modern commercial world that some women are forced to take heavy labors that are usually taken by men due to some social circumstances, one of which may be the overplay of individual freedom, and as a result of long practice, the women may change their views of the world, the relationships between human beings and their personality may change to become harder, more competitive while losing more soft side of the feminine energy, which is against the softness of God's nature.

We must also be aware as an individual human being, each of us has the Yin Yang energies installed in us, reflected as characteristics of feminine and masculine; how these two energies play out in an individual's life and how much impact they would have on the physical appearances it would be all up to the Creator; as fellow humans we would only need to accept and appreciate the abundant life forms brought to us by the Opulence of the Creator as long as the principles of Equality and Freedom are kept in balance in social encounters.

All the four principles of the Heavenly Law of Balance are always working at the same time in nature, one or two may have more binding effect than the others at a time or in different circumstances. No matter as an individual, or a social entity, when we experience sufferings and chaos, it is always an indication that something in practice is in discord, violating the heavenly principles, and this 'something' can either originate from ourselves or from the environment we are living in, and a change or an adjustment is required if further damages are to be avoided. And in the Green Earth Life everyone would need to be aware that the ultimate Law and Principles that govern human societies for a life of ease and peace for the whole matter more than the same Law and Principles of local and parts when comes to a decision making; so anyone would need to be ready for compromises as a part in front of the whole in respect to all affairs domestic or international alike; individual or collective group alike, whoever acts against it can only taste the bitterness and eventually be thrown under the wheel of history since Law of Balance is the universal law.

Definitions and Conceptual Comprehension Under Green Earth Life

Green - a symbol of Life Eternal; living a life surrounded by trees and vegetations with colors; a view that believes life is endless circles of interwoven spirits clothed with different forms that sustain themselves by receiving and supplying energy within the circles in nature, inclusive of humans, animals, plants, water, air, earth and all other visible, invisible living beings

Sustainable - an approach of social economy that organizes human activity within the ecosystems of the earth life with regards to production, service and consumption aiming to sustain a full and healthy human life, a healthy human society, not for material hoarding. It is not understood that a resource has endless supply and can be used for free at the perception of human's mind therefore to organize human activity for excessive exploitation and consumption. Since in nature nothing is free for exploitation, it is always an exchange between giving and receiving. A healthy human body, a healthy human society can only be obtained and sustained by following the natural law of balance to conduct their activities, in the cycles of days and nights, seasons and years experiencing stages of dormancy, germination, growth and harvest

Rule of Law - the Earth is one whole community, the behaviors and activities of any earth citizen and subcommunity shall follow the four principles of the Heavenly Law. United Nations is the ultimate body to oversee the earth community and subcommunities in their conduct, such as regional groups, nations, any institutional groups. The laws and regulations instituted to govern all individuals and communities on earth must be in accord with the four principles of the Heavenly Law for the purposes of directing energy and resources to flow in ease for the wellbeing of all living beings on earth, instead of being fabricated at human's will aiming at controlling and containing for the interests of parts and a few, and should be in constant revision with the evolution of human consciousness. The head of a community is a guardian of the community, not a ruler, must be appointed by a sufficient numbers of members of the community, serve in terms depending on the moral value how God nature is upheld by the head in his service to the community. The ultimate purpose of the laws is to keep matters in natural order, in natural flow, not for containing; it is believed that the existing laws and regulations in human society are out of date and need to be updated in order to keep things, matters in natural order and flow

Wellbeing - a general state that the basic needs for food, water and shelter in natural condition is met for all biological lives; in human society, apart from the basic needs, it also includes a healthy state of mental, psychological and spiritual development. Note: mental and psychological faculties are of the mind belonging to the physical realm, which can be naturally developed in human environment if the basic physical needs are met, and therefore spiritual development (the three relationships with oneself, with others and with the Divine) is the only extended aspect to achieve wellbeing for a human being. Apart from these two aspects, all other human needs are regarded as extensions to the body, which are extra costs to the body and can hinder the development of the spiritual faculty hence the wellbeing of the human being. And the spiritual health is crucial for the human body's physical health and the full wellbeing since a well developed state of spirit of the body will generate healthy blood cells to maintain a healthy immune system to ward off any intrusive cells therefore maintain an overall health of the human being.

Human Rights - the core human rights in the Green Earth Life do not depart from the four principles of the Heavenly Law, if equality and freedom inscribed in the principles have had been kept so far in human society, the word 'human rights' would not have even necessarily appeared in human's mind. When we look at today's human rights issues, it is simply because the basic principles for governing human society are violated. Therefore If the two aspects of the principle Freedom are being watched and upheld all human rights issues would disappear and the word itself would have no reason to exist:

1) freedom for moving around physically, accessing food, water, air and natural shelter for physical health and sustain the body. Note: natural shelter refers to a shelter that obtained with simple labor and natural materials without severe destruction of the nature formation. Looking at birds, they pick up twigs, small branches that already fell or are ready-to-pick suitable materials to make their shelters; other animals live in trees, caves or

underground burrows made by their own 'hands'.

2) freedom for speech, opinion expression, belief, gathering to maintain spiritual wellbeing

This second aspect has been usually ignored by a lot, however with human's consciousness evolving, people both oppressed and oppressing are starting to realize how important roles free speech and free opinion expression to play in maintaining a healthy, peaceful and harmonious human society and the wellbeing of each member of the society.

Therefore from now on, those who are entrusted by people and by the Providence to have a chance to execute 'authority' and to lead, to govern an entity, be it a local group, a nation, an international institution, are obliged to make available social facilities and environment to fulfill the achievement of the principles and to keep an attitude of service in their daily deeds and frequently have them and their own ambitions checked to make sure all the principles are egalitarian. There is only one reason to explain: anyone who is at his current position should not think and say: oh it is my own effort and intelligence that have brought me success and all these achievements. Remember, God, the Providence, always fulfills His will in fulfilling people's will; if He wills, He would take all your 'success' away anytime unless what your pursuit fits into His will for the benefit of all. A reminder to all who have been sent God messages: do not transgress, do not contain; God is pervading, He knows everything you do, you intend to do; so surrender to Him, serve Him to fulfill your dreams!

Guided by the Continuation of Supreme Revelation to X.H. New Wisdom

Part II Green Earth Initiatives

Holistic Approach for Global Development of Green Economy with an Earth Vision Amidst Climate Change and Environment Devastation

Here is a story: Once there were three friends who wanted to swim in the sea, and each of them had a big decorative stone which they liked. The first friend did not want to leave it behind in fear that it would be stolen, so he tied this stone to one end of a rope and the other end of the rope to his waist; the second friend did not want to leave it behind either, so with a rope he tied it to his neck; the third friend decided to leave it behind on the shore. Then they all went into the sea. After a while, the second friend drowned because he could not raise his head. The other two swam further, and a shark was approaching. They shouted for help while trying to race back to the shore. But the first friend felt so scared and heavy on his waist and moved very slow, so he was caught by the shark, did not last till the safeboat came for rescue.

The luckiest one is the third friend who left the stone behind, he was taken by the safeboat back to the shore; when he got on the shore, to his astonishment, the stone he had left behind now became a golden crystal ball with shimmering lights under the sun.

When the four principles of the Heavenly Law are upheld by more earth citizens and become the binding laws of their behaviors and activities, especially by those who are in governing positions and making decisions on public policies, and when the body of humanity is anchoring in a resting place so that the mind is being unsealed, a vast space of new horizons and infinite possibilities on earth would open up in front of our eyes, then our Mother Earth would regain her freshness, and be transformed into a Green Land with Eternal Water spreading all over the land.

The four principles of the Heavenly Law require us to take a holistic approach from an earth vision when initiating new policies to develop the world 'economy' and the earth life; that is to say many of the initiations and new policies would require nations, regions to cooperate, coordinate each other to make sure we do not make repetitive projects based on competition which would unavoidably make waste of the natural resources and manpower, instead we would look into each nation's available resources and make use of that advantage to organize and provide its services to itself and to the rest of the world. The Creator gives every of His creations something valuable for it to utilize and to play to thrive, only men have closed our own eyes not to see the value of our own but misfocus the eyes on that of other people's and of other beings therefore lead to the competition and bloodshed of humanity. Now this is becoming the past, with billions of souls awakened we see everywhere is water, everywhere is life.

Here are the current realities we also need to bear in mind:

Humanity each year already consumes the earth resources more than four months earlier than it can be replenished. And we know with different countries the figure is different. The Ecological Footprint of high-income countries is five times that of low-income countries. The 10 nations with the highest Ecological Footprint are the United Arab Emirates, Qatar, Denmark, Belgium, United States, Estonia, Canada, Australia, Kuwait and Ireland.

Here are scenarios according to WWF: if all of humanity lived a lifestyle as an average resident in the following countries, the earth resources would be required as shown below:

Country	Resource (#of Planet Earth)	GDP Per capita (US$)
Indonesia	2/3	3,491.9
Argentina	1.6	12,568.6
USA	5	54,629.5

The New Earth Life initiations we provide here are presented in four categories as Symbolism, Reversion and Conversion, Creation, Human Species Management. Some initiatives would need government policies to secure to be fully and effectively implemented, some can be carried straightaway by individuals and groups, and some may have already been in practice only need to expand to a much larger scale and be promoted to reach global awareness and actions. And it is also our hope that these eye opening and ceiling-breaking initiatives can also serve to spark more green initiatives in all aspects of life on earth which be well grounded and follow the route of restoration and rebalance of the earth energy field.

I Symbolism -
Alteration of the Great Sphinx of Giza

The Revelation -
Pharaoh: the great house
Pyramid and Sphinx structure meaning: In line with the fact that the material of the much larger base of the pyramids were heavier granite and above the base it changed to lighter limestone, and the capstones were normally decorated with gold leafs, it comes to that human being's life journey is to transcend from the heavy massive matter world to reach to the lighter, energy world, becoming soft, he transforms from a lion's body to a lamb's body

Pyramid tombs guarded by Sphinx: human beings are now at the verge of the door inside the tomb, craving out, however with this Sphinx, a dreadful beast guarding outside the gate, we cannot come out. The Sphinx body has to be substituted by a lamb's body, the head be cut and laid on the ground, Implying human beings must change the mind completely, to God head.

One important action we would need to take to fully fulfill the transformation of humanity to God Nature is to alter peacefully the Great Sphinx statue standing on the ancient tomb site of Egypt as an symbolic action to show the Divine that we are ready and determined to drop our beast nature and to return to the original state of God's creation, the Personality of God Head. This alteration of the geographic placement and nature change of the creature would send through the sky space to the Creator the messages of our willingness and determination for the transformation. According to news report ISIS intends to destroy the Great Sphinx Statue. This is a perfect example to showcase human's history of struggle and bloodshed: when we acted blindly we might have done something fitting into God's intention partially but could never fully fulfill His will therefore we experienced hardship and brought bloodshed to each other. This blind strife is to end.

Many of the scriptures and legends tell us that human beings along the course of development till today's stage, symbolically we became beings either with a lion head or a lion body exuberating unrestrained strife more than Sons of God would necessarily have, therefore became 'dead' with eternal water flowing away from us, and our lion's strife simply guards the dead tombs to prevent the 'dead' to become 'alive'.

To become alive again, each of us would have to experience to be 'slain' and to become a quiet lamb with softness and tenderness.

The Great Sphinx in Giza means the terrifying one or father of the dread. The Statue was built locating in southeast of the Great Pyramids, and It is believed that the head of the Great Sphinx is a mimic of Egyptian Pharaoh Khafra around 2558–2532 BC, a cruel king in the Fourth Dynasty. On the inscription of a 1400 BCE stele at the side of the Sphinx, three aspects of Egyptian sun deity were listed: god of crawling, god of striving, god of creation. And the inclusion of the three figures of sun god on Pharaoh's tombs became common and tradition since then. With this three aspects included, it also clearly foretold the journey that humanity would have to go through in later history. We know deities were demigods, and they were created beings, they were in fact the manifestation of human's different desires in energy. The association between deities and Egyptian Pharaohs was a representation of a close relationship of human beings with the Divine at that historical time as well as an indication of men's starting point of strife to exalt to the status of God. Now we are at the end of god of striving, by altering the Sphinx Statue to a

Lamb's body, symbolically we enter into the age of god of creation.

What to do?
Step 1   remove the head of the statue by cutting it off without damage symbolizing being 'slain', and put it aside in a manner of dropping on the ground naturally. Leave it for a while

Step 2   build a lamb body of the same scale with same or similar materials at southwest of the same tomb, next to the Sphinx and put the old head on the new lamb body. It would be ideal if this project would be completed by end of 2017

Step 3 give the new statue a name implying softness, gentleness

Whoever undertakes the project he would need to cooperate with the government of Egypt and the UNESCO for specific arrangement. Machinery used in this project should not exceed 30%, manpower and labor are required as much as possible.

II Reversion and Conversion Projects

Here is a memory: Helen was a child of the baby boom in China. Back in Beijing there used to be trees in and outside their living quartyard and along the streets including mulberry trees, jubilee date trees. Birds sit in roles on electric wires and posts and in the trees... In summer large numbers of dragonflies were hovering in the sky often with one or two high-pitched singing of cicadae in the background. The kids always came out to catch couple of dragonflies with their own hand-made net and put them in their room to take care of mosquitoes. Every time after a big storm they would rush out to play and pick the dates floating in the one foot deep rainfall brought down from the tall trees by the storm otherwise they would never reach. Then she grew to a teenager, birds were caught for food, fewer and fewer of them could be seen, then the worms started hanging down the trees blocking their passes, then trucks came to spray the trees, and more trees were cut down for road widening, for extensions to living space for people, more tall buildings arose, wider roads were built, now hardly you can spot any birds in most of living areas in Beijing. She also remembers every Eve of the National Day on Sep 30, their family and neighbors would come out to watch the fireworks set out from TianAnMen Mension. While waiting for the fireworks to start they had to put on very heavy coats in the chilly autumn evening. But now even in early November you may only need to wear a shirt to stay out in the evening. What a big difference we have already experienced in just 40-50 years!

Although the above story was the life experienced by Helen in China, it is a fact that more or less similar stages of social development most of people on earth have experienced, only in some countries it might have happened earlier, or later. Human activities cleared away most of the forest and vegetation cover on the earth which are the source of food, shelter and soil moisture manager and climate keeper for all lives to sustain. According to WRI research, 30 percent of global forest cover has been cleared, while another 20 percent has been degraded and most of the rest has been fragmented, leaving only about 15 percent intact. And according to WWF, WFO, before industrial revolution we still had 46% forest cover on land but now at a rate of 36 football fields per minute clearance we have only an average 30% forest cover. And the clearance of vegetation is happening at every corner of the earth for all kinds of constructions, or destroyed by wars. In some countries in the Middle

East and North Africa the coverage becomes near zero percent, which is unacceptable.

Modern cities spread all over the earth, which have cleared away most vegetations and forests, directly cause the temperature rising; and condensed city buildings, road constructions, sewage facilities further disturb the even distribution of precipitation on the ground which have altered the structure of the underground soil in cities, wiped out many species in the sky, on and under the ground which have further worsen the climate change. The condensed human population and activities in cities contribute much of the air pollution and high temperature trap to push the global temperature up.

It is natural we would need to stop the modern urbanization on building megacities, instead develop small green towns with moderate life style, transform existing modern cities to green cities, change working styles, improve rural areas with green infrastructure and keep them as natural as they are. We must loosen our grips, let nature let other species do their job to release human's burden. Because water and forest are the two foremost elements for life to start and grow on the basis we are on earth, we would need to start from restoration of the basic blocks in the life circles – restore forest to retain and induce rainfall to bring the temperature down and to regulate the climate; flood and draught management through diversion projects to make full use of the flood water for the supply to the draught areas; return large proportion of agriculture land to pastures, bushes or wetlands for nurturing herbivores and fresh water fish and marine life to provide natural food for humans and for other carnivores under human supervision and management

Initiative 1#　　No Land Left Dry Global Vegetation Movement

From governments to institutions to individuals all are called for immediate actions in participating in this movement, aiming at stopping deforestation of the original rainforest, and restoring global forest coverage to an average 50% of the land by 2035. And the ground cover vegetation such as wetland, pastures, bushes, grasses are not in this figure, which would need to be restored to cover the rest of the land interval with human dwellings. This global project be set as a priority for the work of governments and some milestones would be set by individual governments according to the stage and variety of their forest and vegetation coverage to reach the global target.

According to the World Bank, the current global forest coverage is around 31%, however many human populated places have less than 20%, in the middle east and north African countries many of them have only above zero percent. However there are some countries whose coverage has reached more than 50%. In order to subdue the climate change and transform our current self-killing economy, all countries would need to increase their forest coverage to add to the global reach of 50% and diverse their economy capacity. The ultimate goal of restoration of forest worldwide is to provide the base supply for reintroducing various species including large herds of herbivores wild and feral alike to release human species from toiling on the ground to live a life of ease and harmony with the earth environment.

When planting new trees, diversity of species is an important consideration to include fruit, nut trees edible for humans, for other herbivores, and naturally fast growing trees for construction materials like bamboos, some hardwood trees. We know there are several degree differences with and without a tree under a scorching sun, so we would surely expect a big drop in temperature even in the very first years of the global movement

By increasing forestry the following major benefits can be achieved:
- Reduce temperature by satisfying degrees to combat the climate change
- Provide a healthier air quality for the health of human beings and other species
- Keep even distribution of precipitation on the ground for the benefit of the soil and the ecosystems
- Provide shelters and food for other species in turn to sustain human beings
- Provide more economic sources
- Provide natural food supply for human beings, which must be under management
- Apart from above benefits, it will help calm down, quiet human species by filtering away a large proportion of ultra sunlight

Here are some guidelines:
- Countries whose coverage falls below 30% need to bring it up to reach 30%
- Countries whose coverage falls between 50-30.01% need to reach 50%
- Countries whose coverage are above 50% would uphold the rate and increase to its maximum capacity towards 70%

- The 7.3 billion human beings are separately called each to plant 3 trees (a symbolism of full life to grow in a person, Yin Yang Union in Spirit) in the coming 1-3 years and watch and nurture them for growth. In 3 years time the earth will have about 21 billion new trees to start to contribute to the earth life. If we calculate each tree with about 20 square foot canopy, then the 21 billion trees would provide about 400,000 hectares (about 1500 square miles) of shelter to other animals, although the world is at a rate of 7.6million hectares loss each year in current economy course, and the 400,000 hectares of new trees may not be a big deal compared to nature's forest however they bear special spirit of the growers, and the ripple effect of the Spirit from the awakened souls and life they would bring to the earth will be immeasurable

Where to plant:
- along streets in cities
- along any one way public roads. Any two-way public road with more than two lanes on each side would need to have a vegetation or tree barrier apart from trees along the sides
- Along public roads adjacent crop fields, crops be planted at least 20 feet away from the public road
- in pastures and bush lands to provide shelters for grazing animals and attract flying creatures

City and Rural Development Seeking Balance in respect of tree plantation
- Transform old cities into new face with more plantation (trees, grass, gardens), all cities need to reach at least 30% of the land coverage, this rate may not include grass and pastures. Pesticide free
- Bring deer, goats, sheep into cities to take care of the grass maintenance (optional)
- Rural areas to reach 50% plantation including trees, pastures and bushes

Funding:

- Governments
- Big polluters such as oil companies, auto companies etc. to donate, to contribute based on their past operation history as a moral debt
- Private funds in exchange for name or proportional benefit

Who are to labor

- Any earth citizens individually or in social gatherings
- School students in field trips, green education
- Military troops for civilian services
- Employed labors

With more trees and green cover on the ground, water would be retained in the soil; no matter it is a city or a rural land, under the care of Sons of God, not a single inch of land would allow dried.

'No Land Left Dry' Global Vegetation Movement is coming!

Initiative 2#   Change the Working Style, White Collars to Work from Home, Convert the Spared Office Spaces to Moderate, Economical Apartments

You suppose you are the trouble
But you are the cure
You suppose you are the lock on the door
But you are the key that opens it

- Rumi

Human's modern civilization led our body focus on the physical world and speeding up in this field of mass movement which has been generating a lot of kinetic energy sitting on a lower frequency field while our first seeded soul in rest energy of higher frequency field was converted and restrained by this lower energy of the physical motions. In the waves of concentrated high rises of office building, apartment in modern cities attracting so many people, our life style has been dramatically converted from relaxation, ease, color, nature and meaning to an artificial, fast paced, breathtaking standard pattern running like a machine which forces all citizens of the modern world to confine, therefore our biological codes have been altered unnoticed by and large which makes us more vulnerable to the invasion of various diseases and health problems. In the name of convenience of modern life but mainly driven by profit, the modern cities have brought various kinds of threats to our health and the health of other species in the form of air pollution, noise pollution, light pollution, disruption of soil structure.

Everybody must have this experience: in the evening you stay in a room with the light on all the way till you want to go to bed. The moment you switch off the light, your eyes are immediately surrounded with black darkness without even a glimpse of light, you definitely do not want to move, but after a few seconds you start to see the outlines of all objects in your room, and then you are able to see them clearly and comfortably move around with the moonlight in the background. Has the density or degree of the darkness changed? No, it is your body that makes the adjustment on your eye balls so that they can assist your body to complete the command of your mind. A long time night traveler is much more agile and feels more comfortable when walking in the dark than a person who is a long time modern city dweller. Birds and other animals move around, migrate or rest according to the sunlight. The modern city workers are forming a habit of working late and getting up late, and the prolonged hours of artificial illumination in city nights not only disturb the natural patterns of day and night which further disturbs the natural life patterns of all biological lives, it also consumes 25% of all energy usage worldwide, according to International Journal of Science and Research. And a lot of cities are still in a lightning speed to clear the land for more construction use which would need to be halted if we truly want a green economy.

It is already a common fact that the long hour driving between work and home while being stuck in traffic is a big source of stresses to people and pollution to our environment today, and It may steal away the peace of our families. According to US EPA, today car emissions contribute 75% CO_2 pollution in US. And many new diseases are bothering our exhausted body, new stresses strip the tranquility of our mind and emotions. Why do you think we have increasingly large number of people with mental health, a large number of people die of heart diseases, high blood pressures?

According to statistics of WHO, GHO, AHA
- Cardiovascular disease is the leading global cause of death, accounting for 17.3 million deaths per year, a number that is expected to grow to more than 23.6 million by 2030 if the current trend of lifestyle is not intervened

- In 2008, cardiovascular deaths represented 30 percent of all global deaths, with 80 percent of those deaths taking place in low- and middle-income countries

- Nearly 787,000 people in the U.S. died from heart disease, stroke and other cardiovascular diseases in 2011. That is about one of every three deaths in America

- Around 22% of adults aged 18 and over had raised blood pressure in 2014 worldwide

- Over 20% of adults aged 60 and over suffer from a mental or neurological disorder (note, the mental disorder with people of older age could reflect the life they have been through while they were young)

- About 43.7 million or 18.6% adults in the US experience mental illness in a given year, and 13.6 million of them experience a serious mental illness

Our life does not have to be this way, with the common sense our God Nature bestowed to us, we know we can change it. Today the fast spreading of internet connection and IT development have paved the way to facilitate the change of working style for white collars to work from home. By 'white collar', we include all who perform professional, managerial, administrative, customer service, sales etc. who work in office settings but not involve labor work or overseaing production lines in its daily conduct. In a conscious understanding, life is one whole piece, not supposed to be segmented and separated by the concepts of the mind and this is the direction where the Creator wants us to go.

This shift to working from home instead of driving back and forth between home and office, apart from reducing the stresses for a lot of people, will truly serve as a revolution in human's life style, would also be expected to have a significant impact on social development and human development toward a life of ease, peace and freedom; the office spaces spared from this shift of working place can be converted to economical apartments for lower income people to live, and land clearing for more office buildings and city car parking would be stopped to save space for green ground cover for the shift to sustainable economy. Some of the office buildings can also be converted into shelters for homeless people. Truly the existing shelters for human beings are already enough for the population, most of the apartment and office building constructions are profit driven actions which would need to be halted.

Here are the major benefits we would see and expect to see with the working style change:

- Reduce traffic dramatically on road. We all witness how much less traffic on road when on a short public holiday many offices are closed.
- Reduce car emission significantly
- Reduce running cost for business operation and government operation by 20-30%
- Reduce land use in cities for car parking to help transform the cities to green ones
- Provide economical living space for lower income people, to balance the living conditions for social justice

- Much more intangible benefits on human's health through reducing stresses from long hour travelling, working in flexible, relaxing environment at home
- More time spending with family members will likely enhance the bound of family members, to increase social stability

Initiative 3#   Rehabilitation of Wild Herbivores in large Scales and Transform Farm Animals to Feral Herbivores with Global Coordination of Operation, to Build Natural Food Supply for Humans and Other Carnivores. Human Beings Together with Big Wild Carnivores Play Management Roles in The Full Ecosystems of Earth Life. Let the Animals Do the Job!

You wander from room to room
Hunting for the diamond necklace
That is already around your neck!

- Rumi

That is because you are restless,
If you sit down quietly for awhile,
You will immediately notice it!

- X.H. New Wisdom

Guided by the Continuation of Supreme Revelation to X.H. New Wisdom

Is it true that domesticated animals have lost their ability to survive if they are released to the wild? To answer this question, read the following:

... opportunities have not been so general for observing the effects upon our domesticated animals when allowed to return to the wild state. My observations lead me to the conclusion that the tendency is not only to return to the wild habit, but to the original form and coloring of the remote wild ancestor... at least in some species, to revert to the original form and color of the wild ancestor, but they also suggest the possibility that this tendency is the strongest in those cases where the domesticated animal has most recently been reclaimed from the wild state, or in those cases where the change produced by

domestication was the most rapid... I have had the best opportunities for studying this subject in the Hawaiian islands. **With the exception of the goose and the duck, nearly all of the animals which have been introduced into those islands since their discovery, as well as those which were then held in domestication, have reverted to the wild state.** *Among these I may mention the ox, the horse, the goat, the sheep, the hog, the dog, the cat, the turkey, the peacock and the barnyard fowl (p956).*

This is an excerpt from the article *Effects of Reversion to Wild State in Our Domestic Animals*, written by Hon J.D. Caton, sourced from American Naturists published in December 1881.

People are told, or routinely thought our domestic animals have lost their abilities to adapt to the natural conditions and cannot survive if being released to the wild. This is obviously not true if they are set in the right environment. Today we have billions of feral goats, sheep, hogs, horses, donkeys roaming in North America, Australia, New Zealand, Europe, and feral rock pigeons, parrots are well present in cities all over the world and many of them are well adapted to suburban environment over the world. Just have a glance at some of them to see how quickly they can become 'wild' when they have gained freedom, here are a few more records from J.D. Caton's Article:

The goats
The wild goats are very numerous, especially in the mountainous regions of the eastern islands. During the afternoon which I spent viewing the wonderful sights from the rim of the great extinct crater, Haleakala, I saw two bands of wild goats within the crater. I sat ten thousand feet above the sea. The chasm before me was seven miles across and two thousand feet deep. Its vertical walls in a few places had been partially broken down, so that bunches of grass had taken root on the shelves or steps formed in the disintegrated lava, and the goats were clambering about, leaping from shelf to shelf, seeking food. Towards evening they descended to the floor of the crater and disappeared in its eastern arm...They are very wild and cautious, and difficult of approach by the hunter (p958)

The Hog
The most marked and rapid change is produced in the hog by his emancipation from the restraints of domestication and the care of man. In a single generation he changes in form, color and habit from the staid and quiet porker to the fleet and fierce wild

boar... He was so marked that he could readily identify him. The change in form and habit were almost immediate. He soon became wild and almost as fleet as a deer. His body became thin, his back arched and his legs appeared to be much longer than when he escape (P958)

Turkeys
At what time the domestic turkey was first taken to the islands, I did not learn, but probably not very long after their discovery, or certainly soon after the arrival of the first missionary, which occurred in 1820. We may safely assume that soon after, some of them wandered away and reverted to the wild state, and now they are found, more or less abundant, in the forest regions of most of the islands. They have not yet become as wary and difficult of approach as are the wild turkeys here. The natives trap them with some success. (p959)

While below is our current reality:
From late spring through autumn when you drive through interstate and state roads the most prevalent landscapes are animal farms and the crop fields. On the surface level they look so beautiful with the color changing from fresh green, golden, dark green to yellowish brown. However when we start to look

beyond the surface, the colors also change to grey and dark.

Today we know agriculture farming, animal agriculture take up nearly half of the world land, which cleared away the earth's lung, the forest and lush pastures in pre-agriculture time. According to FAO, Livestock farming is the world's largest use of land resources, with pasture and land dedicated to the production of livestock feed devouring nearly 80% of the total agricultural land, and it consumes about one third of fresh water worldwide. Animal agriculture is a big contributor to environmental degradation through CO_2 emission and non-CO_2 greenhouse gas emission. Study shows 51% of all worldwide greenhouse gas emissions are coming from cattle farming and its related production.[10]

Livestock farming and its related production also fight for land use with wild animals and drive them out from their natural habitat to extinction, in return it threats human survival through environmental degradation and food chain breaks. Apart from these indirect threats, there is a hidden and serious direct threat to human's health and environment by creating

---

[10] *sourced from Wikipedia*

unconsciously 'superbug', new microorganisms that are resistant to any antibiotics and cross causing diseases to humans.

In large scale animal farming, animals are raised in confinement which deprives them of natural mobility therefore of their natural immune ability to resist diseases, then antibiotics are applied to them to treat diseases or used as preventive medicine. Quote an article from Onegreenearth.org *"Globally, a large proportion of all antibiotics produced is given to farmed animals - to treat illnesses; as a preventive measure, especially when high numbers of animals are kept in close confinement; and to make them grow faster and bigger…… WHO says this increases the risk of resistant bacteria developing in animals and crossing over to cause infections in people".*

We must let you know that when we were searching for data about animal farming, after some hours, Helen totally felt sick and got headache by the negative effect of the whole picture of the operation, it feels so suffocating that she had to stop for hours to go outside in the sun for some fresh air to regain her spirit.

The large scale of domestication of wild animals happened from about 5000BCE. When you examine the definition or purpose of domestication, it says 'the cultivating or taming of a population of organisms in order to accentuate traits that are desirable to the cultivator or tamer', most of the practice were for profit and trade. And some specific criteria had to be met in the selection process for animal domestication. And we would say the whole of animal domestication practice is against the four principles of God's creation – when humans impose our own desires, criteria on other species, the freedom of natural selection is lost, then their natural genetic codes are altered following the loss of their freedom of mobility, the equality of the right to survive from being hunted, and when domestication became normal, prevalent practice in the world, it has gradually eaten up the natural vegetations nature has provided for all creatures, then the principle of abundance of life forms, diversity was also lost, in the end we are the ones who take the consequences.

Does anyone know that the way of an animal is slaughtered also makes much difference on the meat as our food. Helen had a chance to know this. Some years ago she and her friend visited the tenant whose family were living and raising a few animals on her friend's farmland house in France. The guy had two horses, four or five goats, a bunch of chicken and two dogs. While chatting with him, the guy said, when he slaughtered a goat, he had to take that goat away from the rest of the goats to avoid them seeing or hearing the 'ordeal', otherwise the other goats' meat will be hard to taste when it was their turns. We already know that animals also have emotions, we presume when they see their friends are slaughtered, they would experience emotional eruption, like our humans do, and that emotional eruption is a symptom of the internal system changing which is said to emit a toxic substance to the body that can cause the muscles tight and make the subject feel 'sad'. So we can imagine if an animal is not in a free environment but a confined place and gets slaughtered in a brutal way, how pleasant how healthy its meat can be!

We know we can change this, we know ourselves do not want to live with mind confinement, and if we want to live a healthy life, a life of wellbeing with true freedom and ease, we would also not allow confinement conditions to grip our food supply. So the direction is very clear, we must give up most of confined animal farming, returning large proportion of the land used for animal farming to natural condition with lots of trees and other vegetations, and then introduce more herbivores, both wild and domestic back into the land.

Major benefits from the shift of animal farming to natural raising

- Release burdens from humans for a lot of unnecessary care of animals under farming
- Eliminate negative effect of antibiotics passed on to humans from farmed animals
- Eliminate negative effect of antibiotics passed on to the environment from farmed animals
- Reduce dramatically greenhouse gas emission from animal farming, help improving environment
- Transform land used for animal farming and crop fields for feed to land covered by natural vegetations, help bring down temperature
- Provide new green jobs
- Slowdown the current pace of life, reducing human's stresses
- When more herbivores, wild herbivores are in the wild, natural carnivores like big cats in the

- wild will be thriving naturally due to the abundant food supply
- Transform the human society to an animal friendly society, make it more harmonious with nature
- When more animals roaming on the land of earth, their near God conscious nature will help bring up the vibration of the humanity through their interaction with human beings, and the whole earth will be filled with more happiness, joy and peace

Issues to be considered and need to be well managed

1) International coordination is required to avoid unbalanced development

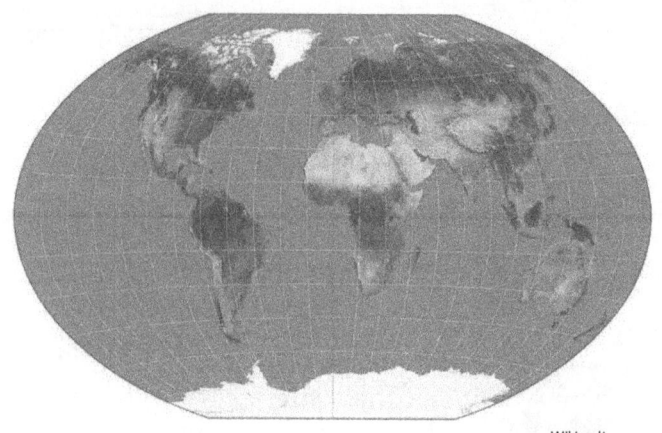

Wikipedia

According to the current geographic conditions, the world may need to be considered drawing some virtual lines for new development zones. The nations would need to work as one earth community and develop and operate in coordination and cooperation, competition would not be encouraged since it is a waste of natural resources and everybody's energy. Zones such as: wildlife carnivore, wildlife carnivore and herbivore, wildlife herbivore, feral herbivore, human dwellings with herbivores, human city dwellings with park herbivores. The principles for setting the zones are that wild animals, wild carnivores should be in the northern countries, Africa, Amazon countries, mountain areas and dense forest areas where there is no dense human population; where the feral herbivore zones can be interactive with human densely populated areas. Australia can be developed into both wild and feral animal zones apart from human dwellings if forestation reaches the required percentage of international coverage. All cities in future may expect having some wild or feral herbivores to roam about, surely would see a lot of birds when trees are recovered.

2) Steps in sequence of introduction
We have to make sure that before any reintroduction of domestic herbivores back to the open fields, trees, bushes, grasses, pastures must have already got prepared for the introduction. Therefore the success of this endeavor will rely on the 1# Initiative Project – No Land Left Dry Global Vegetation Movement

3) Management on animal types and seasons for eco-sustainability
   - Feral animals: goats, sheep, hogs, kettles, turkeys are recommended
   - Wild herbivores: deer family including deer,

elk, moose, red deer, reindeer, antelope, fallow deer, roe deer, pudú and chital; zeba, wilderbeasts etc. that breed and reproduce fast.
- Seasons suitable for hunting must be managed to insure maximum natural reproduction of the species, avoid depletion

4) Wild herbivores and feral herbivores management, avoid introducing feral carnivores wild herbivores are the most desired for rehabilitation provided enough habitat can be restored for them, they should be set as the first groups of herbivores for food; feral herbivore numbers should always be managed as a supplement to wild herbivores as human's food, to avoid massive genes modification to wild animals, otherwise let nature do its course. Domestic dogs, cats and foxes should be avoided to release to the wild as much as possible to avoid invasive feral animals to grow

5) Balance between natural animal raising and other agriculture practice
Human's food supply must keep a healthy balanced diet: vegetable, meat, fish, starch

The land for producing these different categories of food must be kept in balance.

6) Human roles shift, hunting seasons managed
   There will be more seasonal hunting work; hunting seasons will be managed by national institutions. As a common practice, humans will be responsible for observing, supervising animals, preserving natural boundaries between wild animals and feral animals; maintaining lush vegetations and water supply to the natural fields by adjusting it with seasonal change through water diversion, plantation monitoring etc.

7) Hunting Jobs must be done by registered professional hunters who have received professional training for wildlife, animal and environmental knowledge; it is not encouraged and will not be a practice in the green earth life that anyone is free to kill animals even for food. They must be done by professional hunters. To respect the spirit of animals, some simple rituals such as prayer, meditation to ask for permission to kill may need before food hunting is conducted.

We believe all life forms have natural resilience to adapt to natural environment if we put them in the appropriate environment to give them a chance to learn to survive. No matter for a wild animal or a domesticated animal, when it is first set in the wild, it needs an environment where it can learn to hunt or search for food to survive while there is no natural enemy to threat its survival, after it has learned to get food and not get starved, it may need couple of more steps before it can be introduced into a true natural environment where its natural enemies exist. Instinct to survive is part of the nature of life.

To release human's burden, to free your domestic animals, let them mow your lawn

People who live in suburban and country areas and have larger yards and lands can consider to raise a few sheep or goats to mow your lawn; and the sheep or goats can also be raised for meat, for milk as a side benefit, either for self use or participating in local public mowing and food exchange program.

Initiative 4#   New Infrastructure Building and Renovation of Old Infrastructure Including National, Subnational, Transnational Roads, Railroads to Incorporate Underpasses or Overpasses for Wildlife Moving Around and Migration

Mind your drive! This is what Helen has been silently shouting to the world for some years, now openly, publicly!

Somewhere a report worded like "an estimated 1.23 million deer-vehicle collisions occurred in the US between July1, 2011 and Jun 30, 2012, costing more than $4billion in vehicle damage... 200 dead"   We cannot believe, how could human beings with red blood flowing in the body be so cold blood to only think of money loss and human casualties if you view an animal equally a life!

Everyone who drives probably has spot dead animals on roads, and very frequently! And many of the drivers probably hit an animal for whatever reasons. What block you not to see? What holds you back to slow down? Don't you feel sad and trembling seeing animals lying dead, crippled, and sometimes smashed bloody flat?

A deer, a kangaroo, a moose, a raccoon, a turtle, a snake or a bear comes out and moves around, it may be a mum who has a litter waiting for her back to milk, it may be a dad who intends to bring back some food for the mum and her litter…

According to BBC report based on research, an estimated 1.3 million animals die every day after being struck by cars and trucks in Brazil, which is 475 million animals every year in one country alone; In US the 1 million figure is a pessimistic estimation. And just New York state alone 65,000 deer are struck each year. Road kill happens everywhere in the world, but may be hard to have an accurate number. In the light of 1.2 billion cars on road worldwide, our common sense would let us know that the figure can be billions each year. For a long time this issue has not been addressed and attended by and large, and it was the result of human's narcissism as a whole since the fall from Sons of God to sons of men. The ever racing speed of development of modern roads and speeding vehicles have never taken animals into consideration, but driven them to graves. However to a lot of sentient humans, this is not acceptable and it got to be changed! Fortunately there are already some local governments starting to experiment the installation of overpasses or underpasses along public roads where animals have frequent crossings. And with billions of souls awakening now, we realize that without animals being an integral part of our life, human beings will not be able to survive either.

Government Actions

Being aware of the vital roles played by animals in the ecosystems of earth life, apart from some new micro measures to be placed on public roads for driving instruction, which are necessary, such as lower speed limit, speed limit variance according to hours, seasons of animal migration, stop is required when spotting animal crossing etc., a full scale of new infrastructure development and renovation of old infrastructure would be in urgent need both for saving animal's life and for laying the foundation for a green sustainable economy of the Green Earth Life.

What to do

- Underpasses or overpasses are required to be integrated along all public roads, rail roads by governments and the numbers required to be built into a public road would be calculated according to the length of the road and the animal habits along that region. The size of the passes would also need to consider for small animals

- The incorporation requirement of overpasses or underpasses be set as laws and regulations for the development of public roads, railroads both as national laws and international laws

- It also be set as part of the rehabilitation initiative of wild and feral herbivores to the wild

Funding
- government funding
- Private funding exchange for name label to the passes

Initiative 5#   New Human Dwelling Constructions and Other Constructions Utilize Bamboo, Sand and Solar Power, Renovation of Old Dwellings with Solar Power and Sustainable Materials

You see things; and you say 'why?'
But I dream things that never were;
and I say 'why not?'

- George Bernard Shaw

Sustainable! This is what we are desperate to look for, however only when we are able to lower ourselves to become humble, to fit ourselves into the environment we will be able to see a vastness of availability and infinite possibility. If we look at one of our cousins, the birds in building their shelters, they never destroy but pick up things already there for them to use - it may be a twig lying on the ground for some time, it may be a leaf got dried for awhile, it may also be some straws hidden behind a bush. While we humans always bold our 'cleverness', but actually hide our stupidness, show off how brainy we are by going thousands of feet deep into the earth to suck, to explore every inch of the mother to grab, to explode almost every corner of the surface to defile. We do not know what other people want to call it, We would say this is 'rape', this is 'adultery'! Oh My God, this makes us sick! We're sorry, please forgive us, we love you!

And sustainability is always based on 'doing for need' instead of for profit, because profit sits on lust and lust is never satisfied, it is the enemy of God Nature. We see It is a reality that currently there are already many building structures on earth spreading in many countries, especially in developed countries, no matter they are used as residential places or for working spaces, and for long they are empty, unused. Then we would ask the questions: do we not have enough places to shelter all human beings with so many empty places standing and taking up land on earth? Do we really need to take up more earth land, which already endangered our environment, to build more empty spaces? If we could convert some of the 'ready-built' places to apartments, living spaces for lower income, for homeless people, then we probably can avoid further waste of our precious earth land and save for more green cover.

Simplicity is the principle of life with God Nature, which would need to be set as a pursuit for all projects in the Green Earth Life.

Whatsoever, when we need to develop new human dwellings and renovate old ones, we would need to resort to sustainable construction materials, avoiding depletion of the underground materials.

Bamboo in many tropical, subtropical areas, such as in South East Asia, Mexico, Brazil, it has been long a practice that people use bamboo as construction materials for their houses, pavilions etc. Bamboo is the most fast growing, sustainable materials, and has various species. Some of the hardiest bamboo species can be grown in places as cold as USDA plant hardiness zones 5–6. It is said its fast growing rate can reach 250cm (98 in) in 24 hours, and the average rate in normal growing season is about 3-10cm (1.2-3.9 in) per day, and some timber bamboo can grow as tall as 30m (98 ft), and as big as 15–20 cm (5.9–7.9 in) in diameter. It is not a problem for using bamboo to build houses in tropical and subtropical areas where heating is not required. But how do we solve the heating issues if we want to use them in most areas where in winter heating is required?

Here is the inspiration: there was a film set in the background of China's revolution: the guerrilla fighters, in order to survive the siege from the enemies, had someone smuggling salt to them by putting the salt in a bamboo container that was used as a normal water container, and it escaped from the enemy's security check. So If the bamboo can hold salt in it, then we can also use it to hold sand to produce a new construction materials with bamboo holding sand in the hollow calendar, which can contain warmth, and would be a good construction material using for human dwellings in the lower temperature areas.

bamboo w/ sand + solar power + limited other materials = green and economical human dwellings

- Sand   we know Sahara desert is the hottest place on earth because lots of its materials there are sand, we also know sand beaches can be very hot, even burning with early afternoon sun in summer. Data shows sand has a very low heat transfer coefficient of 0.06 watts per square meter degree Celsius, which means it can retain heat for very long period of time, and this would explain why Sahara is so hot, and beach sand still feels warm after sunset. Sahara contains about 30% sands which may be able for the use of this bamboo construction material

- solar power   One of the main constituents of sand is silicon dioxide which is the source material for producing solar panels. Sand is a sedimentary material that is naturally occurring and can be found on beaches or in deserts all over the world.

   Solar power energy plus natural materials to directly absorb from the sun and retain heat, it seems we have got everything. What a beautiful creation nature is!

- labor we would deliberate on labor instead of machinery in all future construction projects related to African countries to provide green jobs for local people

- we may need construction design and material research people do some homework on experiment but do keep an open mind.

Initiative 6# Phase out Fossil Fuel and Enforce It, and Full Scale Embrace Solar

Let the underground stay underground, not disturbed, we have plenty to play with on the ground!

Issues need to be brought to attention and under control

1) When solar energy is cultivated, solar farms must be restrained to proceed for building due to land use and the fight with green cover of the land. Solar panels should be installed first on buildings or as an integral part of the building designs, both residential and

commercial buildings alike, to avoid using up extra land.
2) Pollution released to the environment related to solar panel manufacture needs to be brought under control or completely avoided
3) Further research and improvement are required for solar panel's efficiency for light conversion and device design; Because of light pollution we are more aware of, it may need to add switch to some solar panels for the convenience of switching off when light is not in need during the night
4) We need to avoid the tendency of building extensive solar energy supply more than we need for the aim of maximizing profit in the illusion of 'Free Sunshine'. Warning: nothing is free in nature.

III Creation Projects

Initiative 7# Build Networks of Public Computer Stands on Streets and in Local Community for People Accessing Internet for Online Shopping, Sending Emails

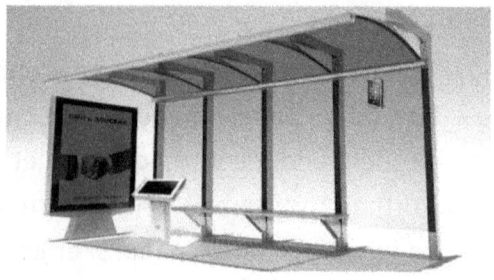

Before the modern mobile phone came alive, when you saw someone on the street talking to himself, you would presume that guy might have some sort of mental problems, but now it is so 'normal' if you even hear someone shouting to himself because he is using a wire microphone to talk to someone else on the other side of the microwaves. Look beyond our physical body, we are all hubs of endless energy signals adhering to a larger complex sphere of electromagnetic fields. All digital devices, when left on, send radioactive signals which form a specific frequency of energy field and if we put them very near us frequently and in excessive long time their active radio waves would always disturb our body's energy field. That is the reason why we feel sick after using a computer for long hours, or put the cell phone near our brain and talk if our body is still sensitive enough.

In a long run it would cause various health problems mentally and physically.

Many people believe they can gain time and efficiency by talking on their cell phone with people or listening to news or music while they are doing physical exercises in a park or in a gym, but they do not know they in fact are doing something opposite. To keep healthy and efficient in our daily life, the health of our energy body is the foremost factor. Our thoughts, emotions, intellect are the outcomes of our mind, which resides in and generated by the brain through brainwaves, in its interaction with the energy fields of the outside world. According to studies, the brainwaves expressed in energy frequency can be from 0.5Hz to 42Hz, and the normal state of the world resides between 12-38Hz reflecting fast activity represented by problem-solving, judgment, decision making, new experience and excitement, all of which are engaged in focused mental activity, and involving these focused activities for long costs enormous energy and leads to health problems, hence low efficiency of daily life. And 38-42Hz is the highest frequency field of brainwaves (Gammawaves), relating to simultaneous processing of information sent from different areas of the brain and rapidly passing information. It is said that within this frequency band where expanded consciousness or spiritual expansion is to happen, universal love, compassion, altruism and high virtue would be experienced but It can only be accessed in quietness. This is simple to understand. Our current modern life is filled with full of deliberate designs that are sending explosive information to specific parts of the brain and with our habitual mind work through thousands of years, we have formed a specific way of receiving and selecting the information the brain sends to us and ignored vast strands of it, eventually we can only think the way we always think, do similar things we always do. And our energy body also contains the heart hub where our soul resides and other energy centers along the spine. A healthy energy body is the outcomes of an alignment between all the energy centers of the body. However with excessive exposure to all kinds of energy frequencies from outsources coming from the world, it is very difficult for our body, our mind to get quiet; without quietness, we would not be able to connect and anchor in the right frequency, therefore we are always in a restless state.

We would always acknowledge that modern technology has brought us some convenience and made it possible for the whole world to come together and share knowledge and information in an unprecedented speed and vastness, but the fast paced stresses it brought to human's daily life and the uprooting of nature's principles would not do any good to the whole earth community, therefore our common sense would direct the use of it to seek new route to fulfill our journey to the Eternal Home. And only if we have learned to restrain ourselves from recognized harms and to quiet ourselves then the human population would grow into a cycle of health and maturity, then the whole earth community would become a joyful experience.

Based on this analysis and the fact that the disposal of digital device parts is highly damaging to the environment, we believe it is not necessary for every member of the society to 'own' a digital device, therefore it is highly practical and socially responsible for all nations to curb private ownership of digital devices and promote the development of networks of public facilities, especially In developing countries where a big market is waiting for development

What to Do

- install computers in local communities, with public stands
- Install cell phones, tablets at bus stops and local communities or existing news kiosks
- Internet service can be considered as public welfare to be set free by governments like the current public road systems in all countries.

How to implement

- It may be economical and simple to operate to have manufactures to provide the devices as a marketing channel and set free for using the service (to avoid other extra facility costs like charging machines).
- Third party can also provide a whole chain of charged service by installing the devices at bus stops, news kiosks etc.

Major Benefits

- Provide convenient public access to internet for communication
- Boost online shopping and reduce traffic on public roads

- Reduce the potential harm to environment pollution through curbing the numbers of digital device ownership
- Enhance social harmony by promoting direct public social interactions in contrast of encouraging individual isolation buried into digital devices

Initiative 8#   Sharing/Renting Network Businesses of Private Vehicles in Cities, Reduce Vehicle Numbers and Ownership Worldwide, Government Policies to Curb Auto Production

For all auto manufacturers, we have a prophecy for you – in an established Green Earth Life society, most cars as transport means will not be owned by a lot people, but they will park on streets or wherever it suits and be highly mobile and in usage by anyone who would need and pick them. It is very possible a car parks today in Berlin, and tomorrow it may park somewhere in Madrid, and next week it may even be seen in the United States; and this means overall we do not need many more cars to be manufactured each year and sadly parked, untouched, and exploiting more natural resources and takeing up more land out of our already scarce green space. And this is happening now.

We may all know now there are about 1.2 billion cars worldwide, and if the current life style won't change, before long it can hit 2 billions. And many people roughly know that car emission is one of the major sources of global warming, air pollution for cities, however these are just the tip of the iceberg when we think of the negative effect a car brings to us and the environment:

- CO_2 emission from motor vehicles and related from fossil fuel burning take about 25% of greenhouse emission
- More than 1000 other pollutants from exhaust emission such as Tetraethyl Lead, Carbon Monoxide, Nitric Oxide and Nitrogen Dioxide

etc. which cause serious health problems in our nervous, respiratory, blood systems; and main source for forming acid rains that ruins our lakes and rivers
- Car painting releases voc that causes cancer
- To manufacture a car, from mining, material extracting, refining to transporting, it produces hundreds of tons of wastes and millions of cubic meters of air pollution
- Driving a car consumes countless fossil fuels which is the major driver of the global warming
- Create a persistent urban rash hour problems and human stresses
- Road accidents and animal kills

When we sit down and think about it: most of the vehicles, after they have done the job 'transport', their mission is accomplished, continue to keep them it would constitute extra costs and resource waste (parking space, maintenance and not in use while more cars are continuously produced for other members of the society). As an average person living in a society, apart from housing, the daily food consumption really does not cost you a lot, but if you want to own a vehicle, that will take an enormous chunk of your income plus time and energy, in some countries the economic cost may count for a life time's savings, and now the credit comes in if you do not have the cash, but with credit purchasing you will tie yourself to work hard to serve it back with interest, and more, this credit purchasing means you 'authorize' and encourage the car manufacturer to overdraft our mother earth by over exploiting her materials. I heard someone said 'a car really is an Iron monster that eats up everything including sucking our own blood'. And to the billions of animals killed on road each year, these moving iron boxes are definitely monsters! This is self killing and it got to be changed! But we also know in the current reality we still need to drive a car.

Then our mind would start to wonder, if there is a car renting service system where you can conveniently pick up a car and drop it wherever you need to, and save yourself every burden to own one, that would be an ideal option for the majority of the population and for the environment as well. And we know a lot of people have been longing for the change only have not found the best service yet. And we say this is possible and it is coming

As in previous sections we mentioned, and the Timeless Wisdom tells us that the root cause of most of our problems and issues in our society is from the 'possession' desire, we are used to containing everything. If we want to solve the problems, find solutions for the issues, we would need to drop this possession desire and containing tendency step by step, and we see disowning vehicles is the right place for us to start this trend. Only when we let go the desire of containing, possession which are blocking energies that take up a lot of space in our body and the body of humanity, we will spare rooms to embrace true freedom, and we will also spare space for the whole earth ecosystems to function.

What and How to do

- A new car renting business network can be born by registering both car owners and non car owners for car sharing with low renting fees going to car owners, the business charges a fee for management and monitoring

- The cars are naturally stationed at the home of owners as usual, but due to its mobility, owners should expect different cars most of the time may come home, and sometimes may not have one at home, but at nearby; and for non-owners, they can pick up any car available nearby and use it by paying a standard fee, and drop it anywhere it needs to.

- The purpose of the business running is for maximizing the usage hours for each car produced through car owners sharing their cars while not losing the convenience of having a car available for use whenever it is in need, not for maximizing profit, same for car owners, otherwise the spirit of the business will get lost and the convenience of having a car will also be lost

- Car maintenance fees such as minor repairs which are not covered by insurance can be included in the management fees charged by the business to make it simple since cars may always run far away from the owners

- Car owners in this network are actually investors to expect to drive a car for free and meanwhile to have some supplementary income. This is the first step and it may or may not last for a few years before a smooth running car sharing network shapes from nationwide to worldwide when time is mature which means people are ready for complete disowning cars; eventually there may be much few people owning cars but a lot of people can drive a car when it is in need. Then the true freedom will come in handling transport for the society.

By observing, If we presume the actual hours for each person to use a car everyday is 3 hours, and it may be less in reality, then each car can serve 8 people in a day (in a global prospect), which means, based on the current demand, our current need for the number of cars is about eight times less. This would be a huge difference in solving all the problems arising from the existence of modern motor vehicles, the iron monsters

- The bigger the network becomes the more natural, more functioning the system will be. The success of this operation will and should be marked by the unbroken convenience of using a car by the members, not profit

- We see this could happen in a rapid pace if governments give more support for this operation

Relative Issues and support needed from national governments and society for this initiative

- Governments may need to update and lift some restrictions on car registrations
- Car manufactures may, may not need to remodel lock system for universal lock such as use a code for new car manufacture
- Lock system for old cars can be reinstalled by car repairs or the network business may take care of it.
- Some auto manufacturers would need to get prepared to transit their business to other sectors or to become one of the car sharing networks themselves since few new cars will be needed each year in future trend

Major Benefits
- New transport model for green sustainable economy
- Curb the total numbers of motor vehicles on road to reduce rash hour problems

- Reduce stresses on people who drive between work and home with less intense rash hours
- Curb the trend for demanding more new cars to be manufactured
- Curb auto manufacture industry to reduce natural resource waste and pollution
- Curb the public demand for more roads to be constructed which is crucial for halting land clearing
- Reduce fossil fuel consumption from motor vehicles
- Reduce green house effect and air pollution from car emissions
- Reduce car accidents
- Reduce animal kills on road
- A crucial role to change human's lifestyle from a stressful one to a relaxing one by releasing the burden related to owning a car

We see this could be realized in not very long time since we have got all the hardware conditions with today's network and technology spreading, only if the mind of people is unlocked!

Initiative 9#   Natural Water Diversion Projects to Subdue Global Climate Change

Project 1) Sahara Desert Transformation to a Diverse Land of Lakes, Palm Trees, Bushes and Oasis, forests with A Holistic Plan to Involve Multiple Partners – crucial project for bringing down global temperature and subduing climate change and transforming the world economy

The concept is to tap into and break the unnatural pattern of the weather in Sahara, through projects utilizing the local resources available in rich to induce natural rainfalls back to the land, return Sahara to its natural state for a diverse life and green economy

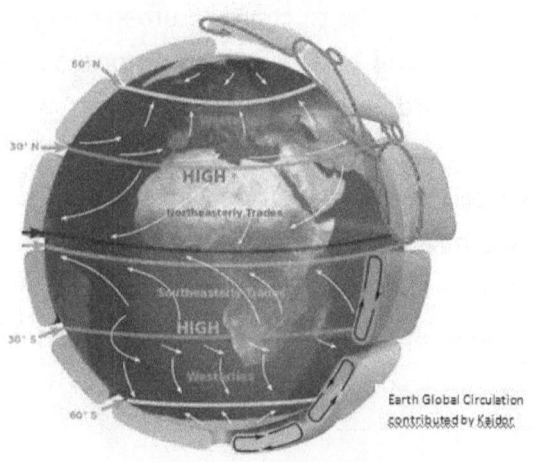

Earth Global Circulation contributed by Kaidor

The map shows the major and strong atmospheric circulations at its upper altitude because of the rotation of the earth. And below this altitude there are subcirculations between lands and the oceans where the winds and breezes form, and rains and storms usually come from. When the vegetation cover on the land is gone, the sunrays directly penetrate the earth ground, the radiation and heat reflect back to the atmosphere to make the air very dry, temperature going up high and air pressure high, at this point to some extent, the hot air over the land has almost no movement and the air front from the sea becomes weaken in front of the hot dry air from the land, there is no air circulation, a trap with a lot of heat energy is formed which behaves like an invisible strong magnetic field that swallows all matters. This is what likely happens to the North Africa and the Arabic Peninsula. When you look at the geographic locations, both of them are surrounded by the Atlantic ocean, Mediterranean Sea and Indian Ocean which produce tons of evaporation from the source waters, how come there is not enough moisture being sent to the inland to form rainclouds? Breaking the trap of the pattern is the key to bring rainfalls to Saharah desert.

As we know the global warming leads to an alarming rate of ice melting at the arctic. According to Nasa, the arctic ice melting may be caused by a complex of factors, but the growingly warmer ocean currents formed from the tropical areas caused by human activity flowing to the arctic is warming up Arctic Ocean and the north seas and causing the perennial sea ice melting at 9% every decade from 1990s and is accelerating; the melting season from spring to fall gets longer, so those floating ice gets melting quicker, that is why island countries and coastal areas are experiencing sea level rising. Sea ice at the poles hold a crucial role in maintaining the earth temperature: the ice reflects 90% of the sun's radiation and heat into the atmosphere and space to prevent the polar ice melting and the polar oceans warming, but the dark arctic ocean absorb 90% of sunrays with heat and radiation. So it is crucial for us to keep the global temperature low to avoid polar ice melting. Hence it is so important for every one of earth citizens, especially corporate operations and government policy makers to take immediate actions and make sure everything we do coherent with nature, sustainable and organic, and down to earth keep the temperature down.

We know there used to be megalakes and large oasis in North Africa around 5000 years ago, and did not cease to exist till around 1000 years ago. And the revelations to X.H. New Wisdom told us we can return the natural land conditions with lakes, palm trees, bushes, oasis and forest if we tackle this issue from the root and let the nature do its work. This initiative will be a large comprehensive project that sets an example for a true green sustainable development model minimizing any possible pollution. This project involves subprojects following a holistic approach that requires multi-partners including governments, designing, research, wildlife conservation, management and labor etc. and the project itself would bring a multitude benefits for local communities and the whole earth community in the fields of climate management, natural resource utilization, jobs for local labors, releasing human's burden, green jobs for international source, new construction materials etc.

The countries in the Sahara Desert:
Algeria, Chad, Egypt, Libya, Mali, Mauritania,
Sudan and Niger
Average temperature in summer 104F (40°C) in the desert

There will be three phases:

Phase 1#   Creating two or three mega lakes (20000-30000 square miles each) on the original lake sites by removing sands for solar panel manufacture and moving ground earth to form geographical mountain ridges for rainfall induction; directing sea water to the lakes with water transporting pipe systems between the seas and the lakes, marine life to be raised in the lakes meanwhile natural evaporation occurs, hopefully three lakes can bring adequate enough moisture to help form rainfalls soon to the ground in nearby regions.   Apply solar power for project operations. Note: the water transforming pipe systems should be made available for frequent pumping in sea waters into the lakes when the water level in the lakes goes low due to evaporation, and also consider for two way pumping if necessary for reverse pumping. If the salt water circulates there is no worry for large salt deposit, and life in the lakes should be able to thrive.

Phase 2# vegetation plantation period, to plant trees, bushes and forest to maintain rainfalls and bring down temperatures. This period would need to train some animal rangers, hunter education to prepare for the next phase for seasonal hunting; human dwellings to be managed and restrained within certain areas, using sustainable construction materials like sand and bamboo and solar power

Phase 3# introduce back large scale of wild herbivores such as the deer family, elk, zebra, wildebeests etc. and to boost wildlife to thrive in this region; seasonal hunting these herbivores for human food, to be managed. Meat export, simple meat processing be set at surrounding areas instead of inside of Saharah to keep maximum organic operation in this region

Major Benefits

- Bring life back to Sahara, to humans and wildlife
- Bring green sustainable, coherent economy to African life and culture
- Green jobs to local people and worldwide with suitable skills like animal conservation, forestation, training as well as local oriented, like hunting, game ranger etc.
- Cooling down north African temperature would be a direct benefit
- Hopefully contribute largely to curb global temperature rising
- Natural food supply for humans

- Boost African wildlife recovery, return the African ecosystem to Africa
- Gaining experience for the world in large international cooperation with building new earth community. Experiment in Unity

Funding and operation source not limited to

- Donation from International governments, or zero interest loan
- Donation from governments of high income countries
- Governments investment from local Sahara countries
- From foundations, large sum Individual donations
- Benefit exchange
- Manpower volunteering for food, living and life experience

Warning and Requirements

- The Sahara countries would be advised to form an alliance for this project and to protect its natural resources from profit-driven operation

- There may be projects going on in the Sahara region at present. It is advised that any projects in the Sahara desert region be held from proceeding before it is approved by the United Nations for coherence examination with this Initiation and with African nature and wildlife preservation.
- It is advised that no projects should be set in Sahara Region for profit-driven operation but for social benefits and the need for sustaining life in equality with all life forms in this region

Project 2) Underground Water Diverging Pipe Systems Connecting Fresh Water Flood Areas to Draught Areas, Utilizing Existing Rivers, Lakes, Reservoirs, and or Build New Fresh Water Lakes Where They Are Desperately Needed

The entire earth energy field has been disturbed by human activity. [11] Therefore we have been experiencing all kinds of climate changes. The most obvious and immediate impact from the climate change we have experienced in recent years are the severe weather patterns, draughts to extreme draughts, frequent heavy down pours to flooding coexist in very close regions, hurricanes, tornadoes

---

[11] *ref. 2 in 1 in 2 The Supreme Revelation*

occur more frequent than ever, which cause countless damages and losses. One of the direct cause of the severe weather patterns is the naturally even distribution of precipitation has been destroyed by human's land clearing, road building, city dwelling building, deforestation which removed most of the vegetation cover on land, and it lets the sunrays directly and long time penetrate on the earth ground, over some places traps in the atmosphere are formed therefore induce the severe weather patterns. To resolve the flooding and draught problems, we cannot stop the weather changes, but we can do projects that ensure to bring back the even distribution of rainfalls, and we can also direct the flood water to draught areas by installing underground water diverging pipe systems. When the earth surface has more vegetation cover withholding precipitation in even then the weather patterns will be able to return to normal. Just look at this picture below, it reflects probably the time some 200-300 years ago, the ground, the mountains, everywhere was covered by vegetations:

image courtesy of the Institute of Texan Cultures, University of Texas at San Antonio.

If people want to invest billions of dollars to build underground oil pipes to transport oils, then we would say, water is much more precious than oil, and we would also never need for worries that it has environmental damages if an underground water pipe bursts. The investment in water transporting pipes would have much benefit to the green sustainable development but surely cost less.

Our current economy is built on the principle of competition, our mind is focused on how to surpass or defeat others and we always stare our eyes on other people's pot therefore ignore many other ways of doing 'business'; The Creator has given every person, every nation something for development to fulfill the life, only we humans ignore the common, plain things lying in front of our eyes. With these disasters happening, Nature is actually doing us a favor - it forces us to stop, to rethink and to go hand in hand in facing these challenges.

We vision a lot of cooperation opportunities between local regions in a country, and between neighbor countries in the world. In the spirit of cooperation, many flood and draught partners can be born. For example, California vs. any of the Midwest states that have over water supply and frequent flooding can help each other to dissolve or ease the problems; Indian government or Pakistan government vs. any Arabic countries; Australian government vs any Southeast Asian government etc.

What to do

- Build underground water transporting pipe systems between a flooding source such as a river, lake etc. and those of a draught area, with outlets along the whole pipeline system to operate water discharge or supply for maintaining water supply to a large area of the land in the draught region and releasing the flood pressure from the flooding region
- In very severe draught regions where rivers and lakes are in scarcity, we advice new fresh water lakes be considered for containing

waters and a supply of evaporation into the air for the purposes of inducing natural rainfalls for the region
- In a large region that is under herbivore rehabilitation projects, underground water transporting system and fresh water lakes are important for the irrigation of the dry land or natural rainfall induction, such as in Australia.

Just one reminder: Do not let money stay in our way, we can do projects in many ways, because we are men, the men who have hands, who have brains, who have hearts, who have the love and kindness, who want to help each other, not to exploit each other.

IV Human Species Management

Human beings are the main players in this whole earth community that includes humanity and other species and all inanimate beings in the environment. The Creator entrusted us an important role to play in this delicate, intricate yet beautiful and enjoyable garden when He put us in His creation - that is to manage His creation to let it thrive through following His creation principles by enticing the Yin Yang, polarized energies working as one. To fulfill this Divine ordainment, human beings would need to let the Soul, Spirit guide our deeds. However the Yang propelling energy is always inclined to taking charge, to dominating, to overdoing, hence has trained the human body with lust, feed it with ungodly nature; and in religious settings, a demigod charged with full Yang energy would lead humanity discord from the four principles of God creation. To change this trend, we would have to abandon that demigod, work on ourselves, return Yin Yang Balance in our body, return Yin Yang balance in the body of humanity to let our Spirit, our God Nature out shine. Thus we would need to execute self-management with these Yin Yang energy working as one guided by the principles. Without the self-management as one species, applying the four principles of the Heavenly Law, we will not be able to manage other species, thus the whole God creation will not be able to recover to its natural order, and God, the Creator has patiently been giving us thousands of years for self-rectification and if we continue to fail, continue to ignore the creation principles in our worldly affairs, He will have to take in charge. And it is happening…

Quietness is the state where the higher consciousness can be accessed and expanded.

Meditation can help us to get to that state, and it is the Supreme Tool to reach the state and cannot be substituted by any forms of spiritual practices such as yoga, taichi, or other forms that engage active body movements. Giving yourself some private time to stay quiet is important to have a balanced life. There is a full instruction for how to live a life of full being in the book '2 in 1 in 2 The Supreme Revelation Part II The Decoding'.

Education is crucial for the transformation of the whole humanity. But we should not fall in the trap of the past that a lengthy training program has to be developed to 'train' people to be spiritual; every one of us is a spiritual being at the core after all. This transformation is about undusting the overdoing and the old binding beliefs, is about guiding people to 'being', not to 'doing', to lose the grip from the mind; a lengthy training program can only lead to the opposite which will not release our body, but add another new layer of dust. Workshops, spiritual practice gatherings, slow motion Yoga, Taichi are recommended for accessing the state of quietness.

Jesus said, *"The angels and the prophets will come to you and give you those things you (already) have. And you too, give them those things which you have, and say to yourselves, 'When will they come and take what is theirs?'"*

When we are able to enter the state of quietness, a lot of distractions from the physical world would start to stay away from the center of the energy field of our body, and at this point we would be able to sense more messages just from the same environment surround us, our consciousness would be able to expand; when our consciousness expands we would start to feel more connections with ourselves, with other people, with other species, with the whole environment, then our vision would be able to expand, our conscious eye would see things as if we were standing in the space looking over the earth, and this would enable us to put our human species at the right position in this earth life circle, and then we will be able to fulfill our Divine ordainment as a manager of His Whole Creation

Initiative 10# Wholeness Wellbeing Public Education, Full Being Education in Family, in Schools and in Public Entertainment

The concept or formula needs to be rooted in humanity through various practice and education:

**Spiritual wellbeing + physical wellbeing = full being
Full being leads to peace, freedom, happiness**

What to do

1) whole society engagement to facilitate the change
   - Fewer working hour practice and regulations, towards 4 hours a day; shift working hours for more people stay in employment. 4 hour working can start from nonlabor workforce for people who apply mind engagement in their daily work
   - Fund and promote spiritual awakening facilitates and services
   - Public media promote spiritual practice programs
   - Clinics and hospitals choose relaxation music to play at waiting rooms, instead of news and

other programs. Relaxation music plays important roles in healing which can save on medicines
- Meditation be set as everyday routine for schools and colleges
- Every person joins at least one way of spiritual practices, at home or joining in group practice
- Restrain entertainment programs which disseminate hatred, killing, violence.

2) volunteer programs

Anyone can initiate and participate in volunteering programs for the environment, for humanity welfare and animal welfare to connect with nature and other social members when needed

3) Life Trees Program, a life time education and engagement for families

For every new born, the family would plant 3 new trees for the baby, watch and nurture them for growing into maturity. These 3 trees together is a symbol of the baby's life – the Yin Yang and the Spirit.

How it works:

- Select 3 trees of any kind, different or same, fruit frees or simple leaves, decide which represents which, ie. one for Yin energy, one for Yang energy, and one for the Spirit
- Select the right places you would want to plant the trees, then take actions
- When you plant the trees, give a prayer and wish for healthy growth for both the child's life and the trees'
- After you plant them always take care of them in the first a few weeks or months depending on the species. Gradually when the trees get rooted, you do not need to put much attention anymore on them physically, but put your thoughts on them, frequent check them. You would always link them to the yin yang energy and spirit in your child, check the balance of your child's life
- Take the child to see the trees frequently all the way till they grow up and the child can do themselves.
- We assume, if any of the trees you plant for the child get healthy problems, you would also need to check about your child's healthiness for growing into a full being

The belief: your thought energy of a balanced life projects both on the trees and the child, and you also look after them, put your attention on them, and includes the thought of the child when he grows up. At the subtle energy level they transmit the healthy energy to each other, influence each other and grow healthy.

Reminder: every step of this program would need the family to attend personally, no substitution should be made, such as paying someone to do it for you, which does not work for this program.

Initiative 11# Human Population Must Be Brought Under Management, Human Species Must Fit in The Life Circle in The Earth Ecosystems, Equality and Freedom Principles Must Be Applied in The Larger Earth Community

Earth life circle is broken by humans
More and more people are now aware that as a species, human beings are not independent to survive on the intricate unlimited spheres of ecosystem on

earth. Without using a professional definition on ecosystem, just by observing the nature, we know everything feeds on something else by giving something they produce and include the body after they die; even lions, the top predators of the animal world when they die will leave their bodies for scavengers and decomposers to consume. And this is a natural healthy process. As one block of the ecosystem, human beings should not have any exceptions in fitting into this system and follow the same rule of giving and consuming; as a manager of the system, human beings do have a uniqueness that the Creator bestowed us, that is the Yin Yang polarized energies in us which would enable us to execute our management role by making adjustment in terms of the number and quality within the ecosystem. To properly apply the Yin Yang polarized energies in practice, we would need to focus our mind on the ultimate principle that holds the Yin Yang entity while our eyes vision both of them in the entity in order to make balanced strides; and so far the majority of human individuals and entities in society have been playing only as one energy at a time and eyeing to each other only, therefore fights have always been experienced, most likely all the propelling Yang energies in different entities in this intricate spheres of world clash all the time.

In August, the world's major media like the Guardian, CBS, Huffington Post reported according to the Global Footprint Network records that on August 13, humanity already consumed the earth resources by reaching the Overshoot Day, which means with current human population and lifestyle 1.6 earth is needed to feed the 7.3 billion people, and in each year the date moves earlier than the previous. The warnings were already there when The Overshoot Day was reached in the 1970s.

All in all, the human population is depleting our planet's natural resources at a rate faster than what is needed for those resources to be replenished, putting all lives on earth in danger. In Chinese, when people ask about a family size, the question is: how many mouths are there in your family? We human species managed to develop ourselves to a state that does not just require mouth feeding but also the supply for a whole complex of lifestyle, and we did not put anything back into the earth life circle, the ecosystem as required being a block of the circle as other species do; on the contrary we give back a lot of wastes being thrown on the earth, which cannot be digested at all by other blocks in the natural process. No matter you want to admit it or not, it is already a painful fact that human species are becoming an invasive species if we look at all the destructions we have done to the environment and the definition on it by USDA: **Invasive species** are plants, animals, or pathogens that are non-native (or alien) to the ecosystem under consideration and whose introduction causes or is likely to cause harm. Someone may want to argue that an invasive species is not native, must be introduced to a native place, but we humans are native. Well, we would say unfortunately there was an 'Almighty Hand' that had been leading humanity to 'a land where we reside as an alien'.

Now we would like to invite you close your eyes, imagine yourself fly up into the sky, farther and farther till when you turn around the entire planet earth is in your vision, and now you see an ancient earth covered with palm trees, lakes, dinosaurs moving around, then move your eyes forward, an endless dense forest appearing in front of your eyes, then the forest becomes less dense, at intervals with land, you see animals moving on the ground, in the oceans, and further forward, now you see human ancestors in a gathering, at that moment a sudden black swirl storm gusting in with sharp sounds... then everything seems normal, however you know something has changed... Now slowly open your eyes.

Genesis 12
Now the Lord said to Abram, 'Go from your country and your kindred and your father's house to the land that I will show you. 2I will make of you a great nation, and I will bless you, and make your name great, so that you will be a blessing. 3I will bless those who bless you, and the one who curses you I will curse; and in you all the families of the earth shall be blessed.'

A trial was put on Abraham; the lord asked him to sacrifice his son Issac in exchange for the lord's favor, but Abraham failed the trial by obeying the lord and prepared to sacrifice his own son's life without shame and heart. With this failed trial, the God nature was lost by breaking the kindred relationship in our flesh ancestors, a perfect example of selfishness for obtaining self-gain on the sacrifice of other people's life, even without hesitation on his own son; this is the patriarch of the so called 'selected people'. Hang on, is this a twist about the three relationships in the Eternal Family of loving yourself, loving others and loving God?

How could humanity not follow the example set by the patriarch? At this point humanity became an alien to reside on the native land God has created. And after this event, the lord came to Abraham,

Genesis 22.17
'By myself I have sworn, says the Lord: Because you have done this, and have not withheld your son, your only son, 17I will indeed bless you, and I will make your offspring as numerous as the stars of heaven and as the sand that is on the seashore. And your offspring shall possess the gate of their enemies, 18and by your offspring shall all the nations of the earth gain blessing for themselves, because you have obeyed my voice.'

And we say we would rather not have had this blessing. Our common sense tells us the Earth as a mass material body has limited space within its boundary, how can it hold human species ever enlarging as many as the unlimited number of space stars? Misleading! Lier! Truly the Creator did/does not want us have more children and He made this very clear by making Abraham's wife and Issac's wife barren, and expressed this also through Jesus mouth. Jesus said, *"Blessed are those who have heard the word of the Father and have truly kept it. For there will be days when you will say, 'Blessed are the womb which has not conceived and the breasts which have not given milk.'"* And this is the time now we are experiencing.

Below is the statistics and projection of the current and future world population by United Nations:

	Now	By 2030	By 2050
World Population	7.3 billion	8.5 billion	9.7 billion
Birth (year)	135 million		
Death (year)	56 million		
Growth (year)	80 million		

We know we have eaten up 1.6 earth each year, a severe overdraft of the ecosystem by killing other species. Isn't this a dangerous violation of the Equality and Freedom principles of the Heavenly Law in the whole earth life? Every God creation is precious, in the Creator's eye there is no preference or favor, everything is equally situated on this intricate life circle, serving as different functionality. The most revered holy man Mahatma Gandhi said: ***To my mind*** *the life of a lamb is no less precious than that of a human being. I should be unwilling to take the life of a lamb for the sake of the human body. I hold that, the more helpless a creature, the more entitled it is to protection by man from the cruelty of man.* And we hold dear of the same in eradicating the cruel practice of killing animals by humans for the whims of mind-entertainment. And we are sure that more and more people will board on the same ship and equally view themselves to other species, and let this guide their behaviors.

With current trend of growth, the world population will be hitting 9.6 billion by 2050. Both from the Revelations to us or from the common sense, It is explicitly clear that we cannot let this trend go further. If we failed taking actions now or shied away from taking responsibilities to curb the birth growth of human population, it would be an unforgivable crime we are committing to humanity, and to God's creation.

Concerns and Advantages
We humans tend to either evade responsibilities or blame each other, and now we say that becomes the past. Because we know either blaming or escaping from reality does not do any help but only makes things worse. We must take actions now, every earth citizen, every nation, especially those countries that

have large population base or have unbalanced birth rate. There are 18 countries each of whose population takes more than 1% of the world population, and among them China, India, USA, Indonesia, Brazil, Pakistan, Nigeria, Bangladesh, Russia, Japan and Mexico's population exceeds 100 million.

Many people may naturally follow our habitual mindset to think that wars are the common ways to reduce population, we would say NO, that is a solution from an ignorant mind, a solution from madness, we know wars bring too much destruction to the environment, too much sufferings to humanity and other species. With billions of souls awakened, we would say the era of blind fighting of Jacob has passed, we have enough of wars, violence, we are tired of these old games that have been played for thousands of years, we do not want these anymore, we want peaceful solutions; and we know if we all work together, the growth of human population will surely be halted and brought down.

In the nature, when we observe the wildlife survival reality, their new born have low survival rate for various reasons, and the most factor, each species has its own predators, therefore their population is always relevant to the whole life circle. Then when we look at our human's survival reality, the issue immediately becomes obvious: human beings now have no predators, and with all the social advancement, we also eliminated a lot of diseases that used to do the killings for natural adjustment. Humans' life expectancy has been extending in the last a few decades and it will be a continuous trend. That means if we ourselves do not play the role of managing the number of the population, human beings will be an ever growing species – and this is already our reality for decades, that is why we have eaten up 1.6 earth already each year. Just imagine you blow a balloon with your breath, when it reaches its capacity you still continue to blow in air without thinking of stop, and you know what is going to happen. And the same, we have to stop 'blowing more human new born to this earth balloon'. Whatever arguments there have been in history in opposition of population control, they might all have held some truth to the reality of the relative times. And with the time going and reality unfolding we believe that many would like to express gratitude to those advocators for human population control throughout centuries such as Thomas Malthus in 19th century and the contemporary biologist, environmentalist Paul Ehrlich no matter what they proposed for solutions. However we would have to say that at the times of their advocating, the voluntary check for birth control could work, but now at our current reality of human development and the number of population, voluntary actions would definitely be far less sufficient to make a difference on this vital crucial factor that has a decisive impact on the earth environment. So Government policies with international coordination for compulsory birth control and execution are the solutions.

We know what is in some human's mind, we'd better give a warning: the Creator did not prepare another earth for this form of biolife, so stop wasting your energy in going to that direction.

There are still too many unnecessary worries about population control, such as population ageing, lack of labor. And we say this is rapidly passing with human's consciousness evolving. There are two reasons these worries are not necessary: the first, with the transformation to the green earth life, human's life will become much in ease and relaxation, a lot of labor work we have taken away from animals will be returned to them and humans will be freed from many toilsome labor work as shown in the green earth initiations; the second, the current average age of world population is about 70, which increased by more than 20 years comparing with that in 1950s, and it is in the rising trend (See below graphic).

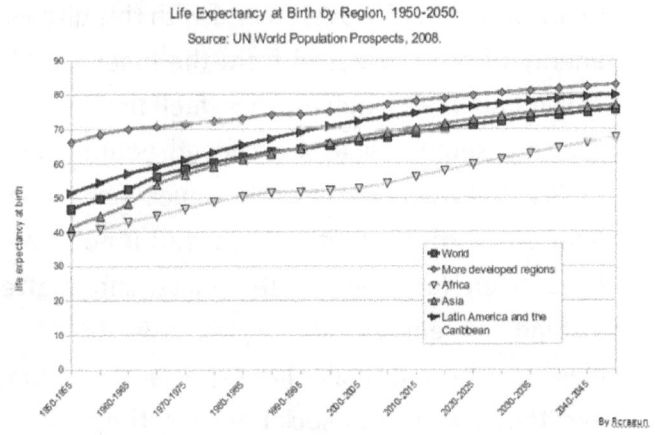

There is a reality in our current human society especially in some developing countries that people of old age are not valued as much as they should be in terms of contribution to the society. In some countries, people at about 50, even earlier are already retired and do not have much chance being involved in larger sense of social activity such as moral role in social education, public services etc. However if you look at the national leaders of the world, how many of them are under the age of 50? Not even a few, right? We believe, as a human, the age of 50 has just started its golden period of life, after he experiences the childhood, youth, early and middle age of adulthood which is a journey of seeking, and at about 50 for the average population, the truth knowledge and meaning of life would be discovered and with this discovery the energy of spirit released from the inner world of the individual makes him or her feel the true life just starting; some call it the second youth due to the reality that the current world values more youth than later stage of life that is because till now the world have been focusing on the mass and matter side instead of energy and spirit side of life. Since elephants have a similar life expectancy as humans do and they also live in social groups, they may provide some valuable life lessons for us. In the elephant world, it is observed that the young bull elephants if without adult elephants to restrain their behaviors and guide them, they do much destructions to the environment and frequently show aggression and violence; and it is common that in elephant world, the knowledge of searching food, water, migration routes are passed on to the youngs through adults from generation to generation and this plays a crucial role in elephant survivals in the wild especially in severe climate conditions where water and food are in scarcity.

Now with this shift of conscious understanding, people of old age would have more roles to play in this human society, and in the building of the green earth life, and we believe this conscious shift would bring dramatic social structure change as well, and become an impetus for the human population management

What to do

- Education on spiritual part of human life, detaching from physical body, free from fearing flesh death. Learn from animals, they are the best models for detachment when facing emotional stresses on life choices.
- Emergency call for a 20 year vacuum of new born compulsory national and international policies, with government incentives. We cannot see any other options if we do not want sufferings from wars, and in fact we do not have the option for wars unless we want to be eliminated from earth. Policies must be transparent, explicit, no deceit. Integrity is one

of the qualities for new earth governance. Specific methods can vary and sterilization can be made both on men and women
- after 20 years, government policy on birth control must bring young children under 14 under a certain percentage, like 10% and keep birth and death rate roughly same
- Introducing strict regulations on pet breeding and selling, and of ability check for raising pets. Pet population control seems a different issue but it is closely linked to human population. Dogs and cats are the two mostly raised pets by humans. Because of human's irresponsible breeding and raising, each year just in US millions of them become homeless and big proportion of them later would be euthanized. It is both a cruelty and irresponsibility by human and an extreme waste of natural resources.

What the possible scenario after 20 years of vacuum on human new born?
If we will have truly achieved no new born in 20 year's time, at current death rate we will have 6.18 billion people or a bit less due to some other unexpected natural happenings. Although this is not a big

reduction, but compared with the estimated near 9 billion the world population will hit by 2035, it will surely release a lot pressure on earth resources. And hopefully by that time many people will willingly and habitually restrain to have babies. Here is the calculation:

- We have currently about 2.3 billion children aged 0-14 years old.
- by 2035, children at 14-0 years old now will be 34-20 years old which are still in normal age for childbearing according to current norm and practice. Then we will have about 1.15 roughly female in age of fertility
- 20 year gap in age in human society even now is not a big issue, and by 2035 it would be unlikely big issues with human's expectancy continue to increase.

Can we learn from elephants, if some people who like to have children around can share the responsibility for child care with their relatives or even neighbors? Sure we can! This is actually the right direction the Creator wants us to go! This is the true universal brotherhood!

Human Population explosion is one of three pillar causes for all problems the world is facing apart from material aggression and religion conflicts. No matter what green projects we take, the earth will still be eaten up if human population is not brought under control and management! And this is a very simple math that any elementary school students can understand

Initiative 12# Return Human's Body to The Whole Circle of Life as Food Supply through Ocean and Sky Burials. In Return It Will Flourish Wild Animals and Marine Life to Supply for Human's Food

When we continue to examine the life of our humans in the earth life circle, as a block not only we do not give anything back but leave waste to the circle when we live in our flesh body, even after our soul leaves the body, the prevalent practice is to either bury it with or without a coffin in the ground or cremate the body in a high temperature fuel consuming furnace, either way is a continuing waste of land and pollution to the environment by the scale of our current number of population.

We understand now that the true life is spirit and eternal, the flesh body we used to regard as life is just the matter form which is always transformable to other matter forms through death by energy transformation. After the true life, spirit leaves, the body becomes a biomass which is same as any other organism and can be the energy source for other life forms.

In the new green earth life, to live a full circle of life, be a responsible member of the life circle, the best practice for humans is to give our dead flesh as energy source to other animals on land, in the air or in the ocean. We know there are sky burials, ocean burials in some cultures such as Tibet, Inner Mongolia, Mongolia and Zoroastrians people in Iran and India.

In respect to our current food scarcity especially marine life depletion by humans, it would be the best and quickest way to replenish the sea food supply and fulfill the will of those who would like to live a full green life by giving their body to marine life.

What to do

- Promote social services for ocean burial and sky burial
- Religious traditional ceremony recovery for sky burial and ocean burial (not include cremated material)
- Regulations must be made for healthy dead bodies to participate in these burials and no polluting materials should be attached to the dead body

We know this initiative must sound very radical to a lot of people right now, which is natural because we are used to the traditional ways of doing it and with our old beliefs, however if we truly want to return the natural order of our planet, save ourselves, we must apply the same four principles of Heavenly Law to all life in the whole spheres of the ecosystem on earth including ourselves, and with time passing, we are sure more and more people will get used to the new practices, then we may live truly an equal, free and fulfilling life.

Add-on

Initiative 13# Dissolution or Dismantlement of the Political State of Israel, Replacing it with A New State of Civilian Territory of Israel with Both Israelis and Palestinians living in to Resolve the Historical Israel-Palestine Conflicts Which Is the Base for Eradicating ISIS Extremists or ISTE

This initiative is an add-on which we did not think to put in this book at all till now when the book is to be released next week because of the development of the intensified chaos in the Middle East. The core part of this initiative was originally presented to the world leaders this June who are in the power to resolve the conflicts, as a cornerstone solution to the whole Middle East conflicts including ISTE extremists. But for whatever reasons, also perhaps the support materials were not enough, it seems the actions taken in resolving the conflicts are departing from the center of the solutions and we see some world leaders made explicit or ambiguous statements to continue to support the failed and doomed two-state solution out of man's own desires, therefore prolonged and intensified the chaos in the Middle East regions, also bring more chaos to the European Union through refugee crises. Thus we feel it is our obliged duty and necessary to include this initiative in the book with more support materials to let more people participate in the decision making on the fate of the people in the Middle East, and the fate of people of the whole world since the conflicts and wars in the Middle East are direct threats to the peace of the world and to the survival of the whole humanity.

And in fact the historical problems between the Israelis and Palestinians are not of their own, but the problems of humanity, so they would need to be resolved by the people of the world.

With human's consciousness evolving, our understanding about the human relationships with the Creator, with oneself and with each other are also evolving, now we know we are all from the same Eternal Family, have the same Eternal Ancestor, and we are brothers and sisters. As mentioned in early text in the book, humanity had been shown through different God incarnations the different pathways to develop ourselves, but we chose to take the lower path of heavy mass led by our propelling Yang Energy and the physical gravitation; in religious settings, it was a demigod, Jacob's god, the Almighty Lord that led human beings astray[12]. In other words, this Almighty Lord can be some people's god, can be a sanctuary to the people who follow him, *"but for both houses of Israel he will be a stone that causes men to*

---

[12] *Book 2 in 1 in 2 the Supreme Revelation, Part II*

stumble and a rock that makes them fall. And for the people of Jerusalem he will be a trap and a snare."[13] And fall will the children of Israel given by this Lord Almighty, "who dwells on Mount Zion[14]"

According to the revelations to X.H. New Wisdom from the scripture, after Jacob wrestled with God and with himself, God changed his name to Israel meaning 'God prevails', in hoping he would stop wrestling with God, stop striving to exalt as God, let God nature dwells in his body, becomes a new body.

Israel is the Holy name, with pure God consciousness, always filled with God's will. What is God's will? The four principles of the Heavenly Law, the righteous relationships of loving yourself, loving others and loving God. As a Holy Israel, a person would need to, in his daily conducts, comply himself with these principles we have just recognized as our guiding laws in the New Green Earth Life; same as the holy name Muslim given in Islam religion which means one who surrenders to Oneness God; and as the holy name Brahmin in Hinduism Religions which is the Spark of Cosmic Energy, a high consciousness in universe. These names in ancient scriptures bear the highest conscious meanings with God nature in them, ie. living a balanced life between the spiritual purity and the worldly life with eternal water flowing through our

---

[13] *Isaiah:8.14*
[14] *A place of dryness, monument, a fortress*

body; however our human beings do not perceive this conscious meanings, but always literally interpret them with our heavy mind work and fight each other for these names in geographical territories, and demonize each other for supremacy. Today we can say there are not a lot of us having achieved this state of life otherwise there would not have had so many wars, violence prevailing, so much destruction launched to our living environment, so many fights, quarrels, competitions around ourselves.

So today's fights in the Middle East between the religions are the results of some people's misinterpretation of the scriptures and their own distorted body by their uneven placed Yin Yang energy, to be more explicit, they are the results of some people's own ambition, desires for power, for fame, for money, for Favor of God.

If anybody wants to look at the world geographic map and link your thoughts to the origin of human ancestors, you would immediately realize that the most destructed areas on the earth are correlated to the origin and density of the human's activity, and the temple of mount was built and destroyed twice, and Jerusalem, the foundation of peace, of wholeness has never experienced peace and wholeness. And if we do not change the current course of understanding about the scriptures, about human's relationships, about the causes of the conflicts, Peace can never befall Jerusalem.

Jesus said, *"A grapevine has been planted outside of the Father, but being unsound, it will be pulled up by its roots and destroyed."*

This refers to the whole Mosaic Law[15]. Also we know 'words' do matter in forming human's mind through photons travelling in the energy world, then manifested in the physical world. The Ten Commandments were received by Moses on Mount Sinai, whose meaning bears the meaning of enmity, hatred and from the clay desert etc. and when we examine the words carried from the old scriptures and the course we human beings have been through, we realized it is urgent and necessary for humanity to abandon the old covenant if we want to regain spiritual freedom, only if we undo the previously established agreement, then the fourth river Euphrates in the Garden will flow again through us, then our life will be filled with the spirit of true freedom.

The whole Quran in 114 chapters, 6236 verses can be summarized in only two messages: 1# God is One, 2# Muhammad is sent by God as a reminder, someone who were given the scriptures transgressed God's

---

[15] *See full elaboration in 2 in 1 in 2 The Supreme Revelation, Part II*

messages, and caused corruption on earth. Just read Chapter two the secrets are revealed there. And this correlates with Jesus saying about the grape wine, and someone who led humanity astray. And from Taodejing and Bhagavad Gita and other scriptures it tells us the Wisdom of life, the Water of life would flow through us only if we live a Yin Yang balanced, spiritual and worldly balanced life, the excessive pursuit of material gain in this physical world can only lead us stray from the green pasture where we belong to.

The Creator teaches humanity through pens; His Words are the Food to grow our life, are the Swords to fight for the righteousness while we are in duality state. When this message has not been perceived, there comes the physical violence between religions, as exemplified now, and in history that the temple of mount were destroyed, the city of Jerusalem were occupied, divided, never experienced peace, because all these endeavors are not of God nature, but of beast nature. Whatever 'holy' sites we build physically, if our body, the foremost house, temple, church, city where Spirit, God dwells, is not clean, not in peace, nowhere else on earth can stand long, nor will be clean and in peace.

See blessings of Jacob and Esau, Genesis Chapter 27:

Jacob's blessing from his father:

27... 'Ah, the smell of my son
is like the smell of a field that the Lord has blessed.
28 May God give you of the dew of heaven,
and of the fatness of the earth,
and plenty of grain and wine.
29 Let peoples serve you,
and nations bow down to you.
Be lord over your brothers,
and may your mother's sons bow down to you.
Cursed be everyone who curses you,
and blessed be everyone who blesses you!'

Esau's blessing from his father:

39 Then his father Isaac answered him:
'See, away from the fatness of the earth shall your home
be, and away from the dew of heaven on high.

40 By your sword you shall live,
and you shall serve your brother;
but when you break loose,
you shall break his yoke from your neck.'

In the most conscious understanding, 'Jacob' represents our body, 'Esau' symbolizes our spirit[16].

---

[16] Full elaboration in Chapter 5, *2 in 1 in 2 The Supreme Revelation, Part II*

Do not blame to each other, the course of humanity till today was a collective unconscious choice by the whole humanity, and Jewish people had just played the role, which was a Divine ordainment; consciously or unconsciously playing this role, the Jewish people had prepared themselves, and they also paid an enormous price for this role, the retributions and It is an ordeal that no other races on earth have ever experienced; we salute to those Jews who have already worked on their own body to become Israel, filled with God's Will. And now it is the time for all Jewish people to wake up and to be redeemed. However this redemption can only happen if you yourself make the recognition of God living within you, and you were encoded the four principles of Heavenly Law, and let them be your binding laws in daily conducts.

Symbolically the political State of Israel has to come down from the Mount Zion; the foundation of peace, Jerusalem cannot be divided, it must be kept in whole, in one. And no political states should be necessary to exist in Israel. And this is God's will.

Since Christianity has made Old Testaments part of their Bible and teaching doctrines and it is the leading force to lead humanity to this stray road, through Jacob's strife, therefore a deep and broad reform is a must-be if the religion still wants to guide people on their spiritual realization.

In the Middle East and North Africa areas, it seems the social stability becomes a down spiral circle: more violence causes more destruction to the environment, more destruction to the environment leaves less Green on the land, then humans there are exposed to more sun radiation, more sun radiation leads to more genetic damages to the human body, then it induces more violence in the human body. And this becomes a fact and it has to be changed, because the violence here is the direct threat to the survival of the world towards self-destruction

Initiation of the New Conscious State of Israel, New City of Israel

Names and notes:

Israel – the New Body, New City, New Conscious State, the Host of Holy Spirit, God, the Creator

Jerusalem is a place whose name has been changed several times in history according to biblical writings, and before the name Jerusalem it was called Urušalim in Egyptian documents. It was associated with god of peace (Shalem) and was widely acknowledged the meaning of 'the foundation of peace, of the whole', The Holy City, Holy Land

Man-made temples were built twice and destroyed twice; if still built by man's will, it would surely be destroyed again, will not bring peace to the land. So the third temple – a Truly Holy Host of God, Spirit, and god of peace can last forever only when men have recognized the truth meaning of Messiah salvation, and man himself, the body becomes a Holy Host, with God's will prevailing, with peace prevailing. Please refer to the Little Book, 2 in 1 in 2 the Supreme Revelation

The whole revelation is telling us that the State of Israel is about the state of whole humanity as explained in part I of this book, not just about Israeli and Palestinian people, therefore it has to be resolved as a matter of humanity; if it is contained and limited to a matter of local territorial conflicts, it would never fulfill God's will – man to become a new body with God's will prevailing, and surely the conflicts will never end, and more innocent people will be slaughtered.

First step of a series

1. Jerusalem, the historical holy city, the name to be changed to 'Israel' to become a symbolic Sovereignty on Earth of the Oneness God, the Creator, an independent civilian territory, a center of world religions, culture and tourism, with both Israeli and Palestinian people living

in, and with local people to be elected in governance, without troops in government under the supervision of the United Nations. It is an independent territory and would also become an open and friendly land for international pilgrimage for worshipping the Creator, God. The four principles of the Heavenly Law be the Supreme Laws in governance of the territory with free elections of its heads.

Expand the city's land area to 777 square miles as implying this is the Holy Land of Spirit, State of Israel, Host of God

A new simple temple which incorporates all world religions will be built upon a time in the near future depending on the stage of the integration of the world religions

2. Voluntarily self-dissolve or dismantle the current political State of Israel, as well as Palestinian State of authority, since the current situation was an outcome of man's misinterpretation of God's message, a result of Man's strife (Jacob's blind wrestling with God and his brothers), and give rest of the lands occupied by the current Israel Government and in the hands of Palestinian authority to their

surrounding nations accordingly; and the residents who are currently living on the lands have free will to choose where to stay/live, i.e. remain on the current lands and become new citizens of the new respective countries where the lands are transferred to, or to move to the New State of Israel;

Note: at first stage of dissolution of the two political entities, UN Peace keeping troops may be needed to keep social stability.

3. Call back among Jewish people, the children of Israel, who live in different parts of the globe to the land of Israel, the New City and there gives a grace time (2-3 years) for people to act. However they should be encouraged to remain in their current residing countries to avoid large number of human migration. Truly the call back of children of Israel is a symbolic prophecy for humanity to wake up to become a new body, the host of God, coming back from that alien field with Spirit living in.

In that day the LORD will start His threshing from the flowing stream of the Euphrates to the brook of Egypt, and you will be gathered up one by one, O sons of Israel   - Isaiah 27:12

Who are the Children of Israel? The answer: those who let God's Will prevail in their life, i.e. who believe in the Oneness God, let the 4 principles of Heavenly Law guide their life, who treat other people, other living beings with equality and respect.

4. This should be fulfilled very soon; there will be unavoidably some population migration. A Reminder: the number of population to reside in the New State of Israel would need to be managed.

And with this task being fulfilled, many parties involved in the Middle East in the long historical conflicts should be satisfied in fairness treatment, and many prophecies will be fulfilled or start to be fulfilled, and humanity will be steps closer to the State where the Heaven and Earth were originally created - the pasture, a Green New Earth Life.

We have to admit, that religious conflicts in human history mostly were and are demonstrated through extreme reactions among those who misrepresent the core value of the true religions

With this task being fulfilled, it would also be expected to serve as an impetus for humanity and for the world religions to start a full-hearted reconciliation and integration process

The Crucial importance of the resolution of Israeli-Palestine conflicts in eradicating the ISIS extremists or ISTE

Foremost, we would suggest a new appropriate name for ISIS, The Islamic extremist group ISTE (ى الموت ف ي الإ سلام ية ال دولة Islamic State of the Dead; T ELMO) الموت ى

The other names the world is using to call them like ISIL, Daesh, both containing the meaning of 'the rising' land in 'Levant' and 'Sham'. If billion times are they called by millions of people 'the rising land', we are doing the opposite of what we want. Words do matter a lot! So we are sure many people do not want the extremist group to rise, but die; and the group's conduct of massive killing, and barbaric behaviors are of demonic nature, ungodly, so they are dead. Therefore, please all from now on call the extremist group ISTE!

It is true that Qu'ran revealed that some people who were given scriptures transgressed God's messages and caused corruption on earth, however as we mentioned before this was a Divine ordainment and the current state of humanity development was a collective unconscious choice of the past. ISTE intends to act as a 'savior' of the world but in abhorrent brutality and force against people's will, it can only reveal their own falsehood. However under the condition of current widespread social inequality, injustice in the world, it can cause confusion and attraction to some people who are not satisfied with their life and with their social circumstances, therefore we witness ISTE's continuous recruitment of people from different areas of the world trying to support them.

As all those religious wars in human history, those leading in the wars misplaced their religious zeal mixed with their own lust for power, for favor of God but infused by their misinterpretation or deliberate distortion of the scriptures and inciting hatred and exploiting human's emotions, so they have sunk into the bottom pit of darkness. Because of the confusion they are so ready to cause by mixing truth and falsehood among people, they are not as easy as we intend them to be defeated, so we would have to remove the root cause which is the foundation of their ideology and incitement. That is why we say the Israeli-Palestine conflicts and the ISTE are entwined in a way that the former has to be the first to be resolved before ISTE can be completely eradicated. With this sacred knot untied, that has been buried in the scriptures for thousands of years, and has been tying up the minds of Abrahamic religions, it will have removed the root cause for the historical conflicts between the religions, hence remove the base for ISTE to exist, by then ISTE will either surrender or be eradicated under the Providence by the world. The ISTE phenomenon is a reflection that the corruption and moral degradation in humanity has now reached its climax, together with the climate, environment devastation both phenomena are in fact serving as a thunderbolt for humanity to wake up and to retreat from our old path of separation to embark the path of unity.

This is the time for urgent but cautious actions! Any doubt or political inertia on actions or old way of reactions can only bring forth more bloodshed and destruction to the world and induce another tragedy onto innocent people!

Jesus said, **"The heavens and the earth will be rolled up in your presence. And one who lives from the Living One will not see death."**

How the heavens and the earth will be rolled up together in our presence, it is up to each of the earth citizens! We would rather to see a totally transformed Green Earth emerge in front of our eyes where all the citizens - humans, animals, plants alike are thriving and living in peace and ease, just like living in heaven, not the other end.

And we see this is the last chance the humanity has to take, and it is like the Phoenix Nirvana, it has to be burned by the scorching hot desert.

The Marching Trumpet Is Sounding

There is an old saying: whatever you have, money or labor, release it!

There is another saying: a person of high virtue fights with mouth, not with hands!
In 2014 on Helen's Birthday, she was inspired and sent her facebook friends the following inspiration. To

those who are longing and heading for the Safa mountain, we hope this could be your inspiration too:

Be a light, to shine.
If you cannot light the entire universe,
Then try to light the earth;
If you cannot light the entire earth,
Then try to light the houses on it;
If you cannot light all the houses on the earth,
Then light the one you're living in,
So that passers-by can get some light on their road!
Be a light!

And to those who are still wandering, or who are around the Marwah mountain, let us do a gratitude and forgiveness prayer:

Oh, God, Supreme Spirit, All Knowing Creator, Great Healer,

Today we, the created beings, gathered here with an open and humbled heart to show our gratitude, to ask for your forgiveness. You are the most forgiving, you are the origin of all creations, You are the Eternal Love.

We thank you for the Sun that gives us day and light, with the touch of its warmth all life on earth grow from infant stage to adulthood to the transformational end; we thank you for the moon that reminds us the night falling and helps us move into quietness; we thank you for the seasons, they guide our body, plants and animals to merge into the stages of dormancy, plowing, growth and harvest so that healthiness always accompanies us; We thank you for the waters, they bring moisture to the air and dews to the land, they nurture countless creatures on land, in the air, in the ocean and underground; we thank you for the forest, the plants which shelter billions of flying creatures, feed billions of land animals who sustain this intricate mother earth that came before us, which make our life colorful and meaningful, and teach us how to be friend with nature; We thank you for the deserts, in the scorching dryness they make us awake, make the transformation possible!

All Knowing Creator, you are the most forgiving! We ask for your forgiveness: because of our ignorance, We climbed up your place and defiled it; we strove too much as we tore the land, we depleted the soil to turn them into deserts, we trampled plants to dry up the air, we killed animals to entertain ourselves, we ruined the waters to suffocate life; we lost your Eternal love to become blind and deaf, we competed each other to exhaust the environment, we made our brothers and sisters hardship, we brought wars to our neighbors. With a full heart now, we ask you please forgive us!

All Knowing Creator, you are the most forgiving, you are the Great Healer! It is in our deepest sincerity please forgive us if we or our ancestors brought any of these inflictions to our brothers and sisters, to our cousins, to our mother earth; please in Your name pass our apologies to them (also turn to each other in group present, say: please forgive me if I or my ancestors did anything that harmed you), please in Your will guide us with softness and gentleness towards each other, towards our cousins, lead us back to the pasture land you have created for us!

Thank you for your guidance! You Great Healer!
We are sorry, we love you, please forgive us!

Guided by the Continuation of Supreme Revelation to X.H. New Wisdom

The Marching Trumpet Is Sounding,
Do Not Be Afraid Your Are Late;
You Can Catch Up,
the Troop Is Ever Enlarging and
Moving Towards Our Destiny
– the Eternal Home

~ The End ~

First draft on October 26, 2015

About Authors

Helen Xinhui Zhu is a visionary, teacher, soul awakening and Green Earth Life Initiatives facilitator. She initiated and organizes the Green Earth Life Walking Meditation Network, hosting the Green Earth Life Golden Phoenix Forum, and provides consultation for Green Earth Life Initiatives for governments. Author of six 'Learn with Universal Mind' Chinese Text Books; Co-author of the series books '2 in 1 in 2 The Supreme Revelation'.

She can be reached from www.learnwithuniversalmind.com

X.H. New Wisdom is Spirit Facilitator of Green Earth Life State, author of the series books '2 in 1 in 2 The Supreme Revelation', Counsel of Helen Xinhui Zhu

Disclaimer: This document may contain copyrighted imagery obtained from the public domain. We acknowledge that the copyrights of all imagery belong to the original producers either labeled or not with the name of the producer due to the difficulties in the access of it.

References:

1. Al-Bukhari's Sahih – Prophets   reference for Zamzam and Ishmael http://sunnah.com/

2. Book "2 in 1 in 2 The Supreme Revelation (Part I the Three Tier Messages, Part II The Decoding)" by X.H. New Wisdom

3. Undaunted Courage by Stephen Ambrose

4. Effects of Reversion to Wild State in Our Domestic Animals, by Hon J.D. Caton

5. Bhgavad Gita As It Is   second edition by A. C. Bhaktivedanta Swami Prabhupada

6. Isaiah 8 (only reference, not endorsement)

    - *The New Revised Standard Version (Anglicized Edition)*, copyright 1989, 1995 by the Division of Christian Education of the National Council of the Churches of Christ in the United States of America. Used by permission. All rights reserved
    - Source http://neno.co.ke/

7. The Gospel of Thomas
    - Coptic version (translation: Thomas O. Lambdin)

- Greek fragments (translation: B.P Grenfell & A.S. Hunt Bentley Layton)

8. Genesis chapter12, chapter22 (only reference, not endorsement)

9. Of Plymouth Plantation by William Bradford 1590-1657
source from http://kevincraig.us/judge.htm
Another reference site:
http://mith.umd.edu/eada/html/display.php?docs=bradford_history.xml

Other books by Learn With Universal Mind Pls.

Guided by the Continuation of Supreme Revelation to X.H. New Wisdom

www.learnwithuniversalmind.com

www.ingramcontent.com/pod-product-compliance
Lightning Source LLC
Chambersburg PA
CBHW020851160426
43192CB00007B/881